Iron Age Slaving and Enslavement in Northwest Europe

About Access Archaeology

Access Archaeology offers a different publishing model for specialist academic material that might traditionally prove commercially unviable, perhaps due to its sheer extent or volume of colour content, or simply due to its relatively niche field of interest. This could apply, for example, to a PhD dissertation or a catalogue of archaeological data.

All *Access Archaeology* publications are available as a free-to-download pdf eBook and in print format. The free pdf download model supports dissemination in areas of the world where budgets are more severely limited, and also allows individual academics from all over the world the opportunity to access the material privately, rather than relying solely on their university or public library. Print copies, nevertheless, remain available to individuals and institutions who need or prefer them.

The material is refereed and/or peer reviewed. Copy-editing takes place prior to submission of the work for publication and is the responsibility of the author. Academics who are able to supply print-ready material are not charged any fee to publish (including making the material available as a free-to-download pdf). In some instances the material is type-set in-house and in these cases a small charge is passed on for layout work.

Our principal effort goes into promoting the material, both the free-to-download pdf and print edition, where *Access Archaeology* books get the same level of attention as all of our publications which are marketed through e-alerts, print catalogues, displays at academic conferences, and are supported by professional distribution worldwide.

The free pdf download allows for greater dissemination of academic work than traditional print models could ever hope to support. It is common for a free-to-download pdf to be downloaded hundreds or sometimes thousands of times when it first appears on our website. Print sales of such specialist material would take years to match this figure, if indeed they ever would.

This model may well evolve over time, but its ambition will always remain to publish archaeological material that would prove commercially unviable in traditional publishing models, without passing the expense on to the academic (author or reader).

Iron Age Slaving and Enslavement in Northwest Europe

Karim Mata

Access Archaeology

Archaeopress Publishing Ltd
Summertown Pavilion
18-24 Middle Way
Summertown
Oxford OX2 7LG

www.archaeopress.com

ISBN 978-1-78969-418-5
ISBN 978-1-78969-419-2 (e-Pdf)

© Karim Mata and Archaeopress 2019

The cover image was drawn specifically for this book by Julia Haines.

All rights reserved. No part of this book may be reproduced, stored in retrieval system, or transmitted, in any form or by any means, electronic, mechanical, photocopying or otherwise, without the prior written permission of the copyright owners.

This book is available direct from Archaeopress or from our website www.archaeopress.com

Contents

List of Figures..iii

Acknowledgments.. v

Introduction... 1

The Evidence from Iron Age Hillforts... 6

Historicizing Regional Dynamics 15

Exploring Dimensions of Slaving and Enslavement 21

Conclusion..42

References..43

List of Figures

Figure 1: The study area in Northwest Europe 5

Figure 2: Distribution of newly constructed HA D hillforts 7

Figure 3: Distribution of newly constructed LT A hillforts 8

Figure 4: Distribution of newly constructed LT B hillforts 9

Figure 5: Distribution of newly constructed LT C hillforts 10

Figure 6: Distribution of newly constructed LT D hillforts 11

Figure 7: Number of newly constructed hillforts and scale diversity per period 12

Figure 8: Distribution of Republican (LT C-D) amphorae (adapted from Loughton 2009 and Morris 2010) 24

Figure 9: Distribution of LT D enclosed and open settlements (adapted from Roymans and Habermehl 2011) 28

Figure 10: Distribution of LT D axial settlements (adapted from Roymans and Habermehl 2011) 29

Figure 11: Distribution of LT C glass bracelets (adapted from Roymans and Verniers 2010: 204) 31

Figure 12: Known communities in the study area during the first century BC and AD 34

Figure 13: Schematic representations of LT C-D trans-Rhenian 'walled enclosures' (adapted from Waterbolk 1977) 34

Acknowledgments

The inception of my interest for Iron Age slavery can be placed during the years when I worked on my doctoral research at the University of Chicago. There, I benefitted from several sources of funding that should be recognized because they allowed collecting some of the data and information used in this book. These include a Social Sciences Fellowship from the Social Science Division and an Edward L. Ryerson Fellowship in Archaeology from the Division of the Humanities. I also received financial support from the Wenner-Gren Foundation in the form of a Dissertation Fieldwork Grant. I furthermore like to extend gratitude to Sergio González Sánchez and Alexandra Guglielmi for inviting me to contribute to TRAC Themes in Roman Archaeology, Volume 1, *Romans and Barbarians beyond the Frontiers*. It was in that particular contribution that I first was allowed to express my ideas on Iron Age slavery. This monograph was completed during a residency at the University of Virginia's Department of Anthropology. I especially thank Adria LaViolette for welcoming me in that wonderful community of scholars. I am also grateful for the encouragement and suggestions I received from a number of reviewers, including Daphne Nash-Briggs, Thomas Markey, Colin Haselgrove, and Laurent Olivier. I also want to thank Archaeopress for their interest and assistance in preparing this book. I furthermore owe a thanks to Julia Haines for her striking cover art. As always, I am extremely grateful for the patience and encouragement I continue to receive from my wife and children. Thank you all.

Introduction

Archaeologists have yet to consider seriously the impact of slaving and enslavement on socio-cultural developments in Iron Age Europe. When slaves are mentioned in the literature this generally remains limited to their inclusion in lists of trade goods believed to have circulated through far-reaching exchange circuits. Many also doubt it is possible to perceive the presence of slaves in the material record, let alone that it is possible for archaeologists to speak with any measure of conviction about slavery in terms of lived experience, social institutions, or cultural ideals. While there are of course exceptions, many who have given the subject attention remain preoccupied with the identification of material markers of slavery (Aldhouse-Green 2005; Arnold 1988; Cosack and Kehne 1999; Daubigney and Guillaumet 1985; Gronenborn 2001; Peschel 1971; Schönfelder 2015; Thompson 1993). Any broader conclusions tend to remain uninspiringly cautious.

With enslavement commonly treated as a mere byproduct of incessant 'tribal warfare', it is generally held that slavery was not a significant phenomenon in temperate Europe before the Roman era.[1] When slavery as a social fact is granted a place in Celto-Germanic[2] contexts, it tends to be distinguished from Greco-Roman slave systems where forced labor had a fundamental economic role. This follows a contrast commonly made in the literature on slavery, between informal modes of social inequality and subservience allowed for stateless societies (and involving such things as ritualized hostage-taking or the social integration of captives), and the formal slave systems of complex states that relied heavily on the economic exploitation of commodified human bodies (Dal Lago and Katsari 2008; Finley 1980; Hopkins 1978; Taylor 2005; Webster 2008). While such distinctions can be useful, I aim to move beyond classifying slavery, instead choosing to focus on elucidating historical, material, behavioral, and ideological aspects of Iron Age slaving and enslavement in Northwest Europe (Figure 1).

The La Tène cultural phenomenon that arose on the northwestern periphery of the West-Central Hallstatt world during the Middle Iron Age[3] has been studied by generations of archaeologists with distinct theoretical and methodological orientations, yet research on slaving and enslavement has not developed on a level comparable to that of other periods and regions. Indeed, no disciplinary perspective stands out in this regard. This is quite surprising considering the way human social life tends to be theorized in our discipline, irrespective of what operators of social complexification are granted analytical prominence. A brief exercise in disciplinary caricaturing can reveal this.

The belief that indigenous transformations resulted primarily from Mediterranean influences pervaded the earliest scholarship, with variations on the theme persisting for decades thereafter (Arnold and Gibson 1995; Frankenstein and Rowlands 1978; Haselgrove 1987; Nash 1985). Characteristically, those operating within a cultural-historical framework tend to accept the transformative capacity of

---

[1] Even a cursory look at ancient sources suggests otherwise (Caesar *Gallic Wars* 6.15.2, 6.19.4; Cicero *Letters to Atticus* 4.17.303; Diodorus *Library of History* V.26; Strabo *Geography* IV 5.2). The Roman historian Tacitus, in particular, provides copious information about slavery as a well-developed Germanic institution (Thompson 1957). However, overcoming the problem of unavoidable cultural bias in the literary sources requires assessment of a wider range of evidence, such as offered in this book.
[2] I refer to the pre-Roman inhabitants of West-Central Europe in a variety of ways, but predominantly as this relates to chronology (e.g. Iron Age, Hallstatt, La Tène) and geography (e.g. trans-Alpine, Aisne-Marne). Such usage has certain shortcomings, though these are less problematic than ancient references to 'tribal' (e.g. Treveri or Batavi), or cultural affiliations (e.g. Celtic or Germanic). For reasons of communication and style I use all without making any definitive claims about emic understandings and perspectives.
[3] I use the following chronological periods throughout the text: Early Iron Age (EIA), c. 800-500 BC, broadly corresponding to Early Hallstatt (EHa) C and Late Hallstatt (LHa) D; Middle Iron Age (MIA), c. 500-350 BC, broadly corresponding to Early La Tène (ELT) A-B; Late Iron Age (LIA), c. 350-12 BC, broadly corresponding to Middle La Tène (MLT) C and Late La Tène (LLT) D.

material culture, even if older ideas on diffusion and acculturation no longer shape interpretations significantly. But, more importantly, this perspective generally supposes that any indigenous desire for exotic goods (like Mediterranean wine, bronze wares, and fine ceramics) was shaped by a universal human interest for competition and differentiation. Especially for the latter half of the Late Iron Age, these prime motivators are widely perceived as the main causes of social complexification and cultural transformation (Barrett 2012; Kienlin 2017).

Post-processualists, by contrast, have generally been critical of core-periphery perspectives that too readily link indigenous developments to external forces, whether economic or cultural. Further rejecting the innate capacity of objects and materials for shaping cultural ideals and social norms, they instead underscore the importance of indigenous value systems that determined how non-local goods, ideas, and practices were contextually negotiated. Nonetheless, 'nativist' scholarship of this kind still grants substantial transformative significance to social differentiation, likely due to the influence of Marxist theory (Miller and Tilley 1984; Sastre 2011), which holds that socio-cultural transformation primarily results from 'class struggles'. This perception is also shared by those who have been inspired by social theorists (Bourdieu 1977; de Certeau 1988; Giddens 1984) and likewise foreground the transformative importance of 'social struggles' (Diepeveen-Jansen 2001; Dornan 2002; van der Vaart-Verschoof 2017). Reliance on structuralist theory (Hodder 1982; Hodder *et al.* 2007) only exaggerates such preoccupations when it grants socio-cosmic significance to the violent excesses of prehistoric life. Where ancient observers commonly blamed 'barbarian' feuding and warfare on essential dispositions and cultural shortcomings – the same sources, it must be remembered, that informed the ideological imaginaries of modern European state builders (Díaz-Andreu and Champion 1996; Dietler 1994) – archaeologists inspired by structuralist ideas tend to overstate the cultural significance of Celto-Germanic violence and bellicosity by embedding these in transhistorical value systems that uniquely characterized 'warrior societies' (Arnold and Murray 2002: 112; Bazelmans 1999; Derks 1998; Diepeveen-Jansen 2001; Lenski 2008: 88). While it might be thought, then, that the post-processual emphasis on indigenous agency and contextual meaning-making has significantly changed archaeological interpretation of Iron Age societies, it is the uncritical foregrounding of competition and conflict as universal determinants of socio-cultural transformation that remains problematic.

Theories and methods that might be characterized as processualist continue to shape perspectives on Iron Age transitions as well. These generally aim to explain socio-cultural complexification in reference to quantifiable economic, demographic, and environmental data. One common assumption that recurs widely in this literature is that social complexification follows directly from demographic growth, with increased agricultural production a necessary (and measurable!) prerequisite (Brun 1995; Fernández-Götz 2018). For example, recent work on Early Iron Age urbanism treats demographic growth as the main driver of socio-economic inequality and political centralization (Fernández-Götz and Krausse 2013: 479; Fernández-Götz and Ralston 2017: 274). At the well-known Heuneburg hillfort (Baden-Württemberg, Germany), local aspirers are believed to have achieved their superior status by successfully mobilizing communal loyalties through the manipulation of shared ideologies, specifically by staging public ceremonies at sacred places (Fernández-Götz 2014a: 117). Yet, it remains difficult to understand how exactly differentiating aspirers were able to convince members of politically decentralized and socially undifferentiated farming communities to voluntarily participate in their aggrandizing projects in such a chronologically and geographically erratic manner. Further, if population growth encouraged centralization and stratification, should we expect opposing developments when population numbers decline? Did the persistence of egalitarian ideals among communities that were contemporary with LHa 'princely' hillforts result from a lack of demographic growth? How likely is it that the abandonment of countless large fortified settlements like that of the Heuneburg was uniformly caused by conveniently quantifiable factors like environmental degradation, economic contraction, and depopulation?

Partly in an attempt to address interpretive challenges of this kind, some archaeologists have sought to examine Iron Age complexification through a comparative-ethnographic lens. Such works typically argue against the presumed universality of economic and demographic imperatives, while also rejecting any innate capacities of material culture. Instead, certain social mechanisms are foregrounded for their purported transformative potential. Thus, it is through mechanisms like 'feasting' (Dietler and Herbich 2001; Hayden 2003; Michael 2003; Spielmann 2002) that aspiring individuals and their kin groups were able to mobilize local labor forces and differentiate themselves within their community. Yet, even with this privileging of certain cross-culturally attested practices and institutions, our understanding of past lifeways does not improve significantly if the interpretive focus remains on competition and differentiation. Further still, the relevance of comparative information also remains to be demonstrated for each context under investigation (Peregrine 2001). It is difficult to see, for example, how farming families could have built the monumental walls, gates, and towers of LHa princely hillforts like the Heuneburg through participation in voluntary work feasts. Such projects required labor investments of a scale and duration far exceeding the construction of even the largest barn or burial mound (Wells 2002: 366).[4] Furthermore, without clear evidence for a prevalence of extended or polygamous family arrangements in Iron Age Europe (Nash-Briggs 2003: 254), it is not at all certain whether the work feast could produce the same level of labor attested in certain African contexts.

On the one hand, this brief overview of interpretive orientations shows how the privileging of either internal or external causes of socio-cultural transformation risks reducing past complexities as well as the interpretive dexterity of archaeologists. In other words, archaeological analyses remain diminished if they cannot tackle aspects of relationality and co-constitution (Mata 2017a: 11). But, more than this, it also demonstrates that the supposed inevitability of social complexification is rarely questioned, irrespective of preferences in theory and method.[5] The notion that differentiation and competition are essential human aptitudes that need only be stimulated – by such things as demographic growth, the inevitable scheming of social aspirers, or the innate qualities of exotic objects – wholly ignores the complex interplay of different motivations and capacities that have always shaped all human social engagements (González-Ruibal 2012; Mata 2017a; Ortner 2005).[6]

Where this concerns the presumed inevitability of social differentiation specifically, it can be observed that norms, traditions, and institutions universally operate to prevent the disruption of social systems. Indeed, the efforts of those who seek to differentiate themselves rarely remains unopposed,[7] especially since challengers of social norms risk eroding bonds with kin and community, something that can have detrimental consequences for groups and individuals alike (Mata 2012: 37). All human communities have always developed strong deterrents for non-egalitarian behavior, whether understood weakly as differentiation or strongly as domination. Further, the Marxist position that elites always manage to successfully deploy mystifying discourse in order to convince subordinate masses to accept inequality is untenable. Not only does this negate the complex interplay of discrepant understandings, motivations, and abilities, it ignores the fact that stratification has historically most readily occurred under conditions

---

[4] At the LLT *oppidum* at Manching, for example, it has been calculated that a single phase of construction required approximately 500,000 person-days of labor (Wells 2005: 57).
[5] The main socio-historical transition recognized is that from a broadly egalitarian to an increasingly stratified society. This is widely perceived as the main developmental trajectory for Iron Age societies (Dietler 1990; Fernández-Götz *et al.* 2014; Haselgrove 1987; Roymans 1990; Sastre 2011).
[6] Recent interest for 'non-triangular' social systems among Iron Age researchers (Hill 2006; Moore and Armada 2011) is a welcome development in this regard.
[7] Caesar's (*Gallic Wars* I.2) retelling of the political machinations of Orgetorix of the Helvetii (Switzerland), whose political ambitions were resisted within his own community, may serve as an illustrative example of this. Another example concerns Caesar's (*Gallic Wars* VII-33) arbitration of internal conflicts among the Aeduans (Central-East France). Within this community, laws seemed to have been in place to prevent the centralization of power; Aeduan families could only have one of their members serve as an 'officer of the state', in order to prevent certain families gaining too much influence.

that are rarely inevitable. Throughout human history, physical insecurity and psychological anxiety are prime factors that can readily be shown to have promoted the proliferation of disproportionately powerful groups and individuals. While both can also inspire cooperative behavior and strengthen egalitarian discourse, the successful realization of equality-based collaborative projects is never easy to achieve, and a threshold can be reached (with or without the assistance of manipulating aspirers) when people willingly surrender autonomy and equality as a way of improving insecure conditions. The asymmetrical relations that often initially form under such circumstances then can become reified into social institutions, cultural ideals, and even personal worldviews (Conteh-Morgan 2002). There seems little doubt that insecurity and anxiety have historically been key factors in the rise and persistence of social inequality (Nussbaum 2018).

Crucially, the cultural normalization of social inequality is a necessary precondition for the manifestation of systems of subservience and enslavement. Yet, such processes are first and foremost historical and therefore require contextual scrutiny. Comparative research on African slaving and enslavement is particularly illustrative in this regard because it reveals what can happen when broadly egalitarian segmentary communities are enduringly preyed upon by often better organized stratified groups (Fitts 2015; Klein 2001: 65; Kusimba 2004 and 2015; MacEachern 2011; Nwokeji 2010; Robertshaw and Duncan 2008). The former are forced through a transformative process in response to a persistent external threat. This commonly starts with the formation of inter-group alliances and communal cooperation in the construction of defenses. Other responses include innovations in the built environment (e.g. increased control of movement), changes in everyday behaviors (e.g. regimented workdays), centralization of decision-making (e.g. management of labor and defense), social differentiation (e.g. individuals and families gaining social prominence), economic specialization (e.g. metalsmithing generally, and weapon manufacture in particular), and the formation of belief systems that assist in dealing with insecurity psychologically (e.g. increased interest for protective rituals and objects, and spread of fatalist worldviews). As affected societies become better organized, the persistent threat posed by slaving greatly impacts how such processes unfold, commonly leading to increased intra- and inter-group conflict.[8]

So, while archaeologists rarely think twice about this strong disciplinary tendency to centralize the transformative impact of competition and conflict in their studies of Iron Age societies, there has been little critical reflection on the exact historical circumstances for these and associated phenomena. Or, to put it more succinctly, a true flourishing of slavery research has yet to occur. I would argue that, just like it would be rather negligent not to consider the impact of slaving and enslavement when examining Early Modern contexts in Africa (Alexander 2001; Klein 2001; Kusimba 2004; Lane and MacDonald 2011) and North America (Berlin 1998; Fitts 2015; Snyder 2012), or Early Medieval contexts in Viking and Slavic Europe (Fontaine 2017; Henning 1992; Jankowiak 2013; Korpela 2014; McCormick 2002), so it is crucial to assess the nature and impact of such distinct phenomena if we are to accurately understand socio-cultural developments in Iron Age Europe. As comparative research shows, slavery is a multifaceted phenomenon with complex interrelated material, behavioral, and ideological dimensions, such that any meaningful archaeological study has to take a multi-thread approach whereby a wide range of material categories and domains of social practice are examined, contextually, relationally, and comparatively (Dal Lago and Katsari 2008; Gronenborn 2001; Marshall 2015). In this brief contribution on the topic, I

---

[8] Consider, for example, how it is far more likely for peaceful relations between competing groups to be reestablished (e.g. for war captives to be exchanged conditionally) when a formal trade in slaves is lacking. When present, however, antagonists have a tempting means for dealing with competitors through an extra-societal mechanism. Consequently, the sale of captives to slavers perpetuates conflict because individuals are not returned to their home communities, which are also not compensated for their losses in other ways (Fitts 2015: 307). There are countless other means by which groups and individuals might exploit the presence of an external mechanism like a slave trade to pursue certain personal or collective goals (Afigbo 2006), often with enduring consequences for the societies in question.

take an exploratory approach whereby I consider evidence from various Iron Age periods and contexts in the study area as I follow particular lines of inquiry. I first turn to the key matter of insecurity by considering the evidence for refuge construction, because this provides a useful inroad for assessing the dynamics of Iron Age slaving and enslavement in Northwest Europe.

Figure 1: The study area in Northwest Europe

The Evidence from Iron Age Hillforts

I begin by looking at spatio-temporal patterns in hillfort construction. Figures 2-7 visualize the assembled data on hillforts in the study area for the entire Iron Age.[1] If it can be accepted that the use of these refuges was closely linked to insecurity,[2] then it can be argued that the latter part of the EIA (HA D=32) was significantly more insecure compared to the previous period (HA C=2). Conditions subsequently improved during the MIA, when an equivalent number was built during LT A (20) and LT B (19). Though the decline in construction is notable for both these periods compared to the preceding HA D period, insecurity remained a central part of lived experience for countless communities in Northwest Europe. While the earlier part of the LIA (LT C=4) witnessed the lowest level of insecurity in centuries, this was followed by a radically different situation during the second half of the LIA when we witness a historical peak in the construction of refuges (LT D=65).

Refuges in the study area typically provide archaeologists with limited material evidence; prominent objects like vehicles, weapons, or bronze wares do not commonly occur outside mortuary contexts (Diepeveen-Jansen 2001). Yet, no clear linkages have been established between refuges and burials despite their contemporary occurrence; even the densest concentration of elite burials of LT A date (in the Rhine-Moselle region) is not clearly associated with refuges. Most such sites are also not favorably situated along transport routes, such that isolation seems to have been an important consideration. Their distribution speaks against a possible function as central places in distinct territories, making it unlikely that resource control was an important factor. Only a handful of refuges provide evidence for craft or industrial activity. Tellingly, signs of destruction and rebuilding have been found, along with sling pellets, arrow heads, and the remains of metal weapons. The general absence of internal structures and divisions, as well as their small size-range (1-3 ha), suggests that the majority of hilltop refuges was built to be occupied temporarily and intermittently (Fernández-Götz 2014c: 107). The scale at which refuges were built, in particular, can speak to the circumstances of use. During periods with higher levels of insecurity, more people will have occupied refuges longer and more often. Consequently, we would expect more large-scale refuges to be built in periods with higher levels of insecurity, to provide refuge to more people for longer periods of time. The sample seems to reflect this: the greatest scale diversity occurs in those periods (HA D and LT D) when most refuges are newly built. The high level of scale diversity for the HA D period contrasts significantly with the preceding HA C period, while subsequently declining again during LT A. This trend persists throughout LT B and LT C, only to rise again during the troubled LT D period. Clearly, then, during those times when people felt enduringly insecure they built the largest refuges, while also constructing them at a broader size-range.

Despite these distinct patterns in refuge construction, and the classification of most as places where local people could shelter temporarily from threats, there are some fortified sites that warrant a different interpretation. The small intermittently occupied refuges discussed so far are not to be compared with the 'princely' hillforts (*Fürstensitze*) of the West-Central Hallstatt world that were often much larger in scale and occupied for extensive periods during the EIA (Dietler 1995).[3] Nor are they to be equated with the

---

[1] Hillforts have been allocated to periods when they were initially built in order to counter the problem that many will have been occupied, abandoned, and reoccupied over time.

[2] I am here proceeding from the assumption that the primary function of this type of site was for the collective defense of people, animals, and resources. In foregrounding this functional use of refuges I am not denying the symbolic goals and effects of communal endeavors, like the construction of prominent settlements (Fernández-Götz 2014b; Fernández-Götz and Krausse 2013; Gerritsen and Roymans 2006). Considerations of communal identity and cohesion are certainly important, but such objectives could be achieved in other ways as well. In other words, refuges functioned primarily for defensive purposes, even if their construction and use may also have had ideological aims and consequences.

[3] This category of Ha D-LT A defended sites is described by Fernández-Götz as 'large collective centres' (2014c: 116). In the study area, the Titelberg and Wallendorf hillforts in the Rhine-Moselle region are the largest at *c.* 40 ha.

large defended settlements (*oppida*) of the LIA that were comparable in size to the earlier princely hillforts (Moore *et al.* 2013).[4] The latter could be quite extensive in scale, and commonly provide archaeologists with evidence for intensive craft production. As noted, the rise of this type of settlement tends to be explained in terms of demographic growth and political centralization. However, if these large-scale hillforts formed an integrated settlement system with the far more numerous smaller refuges – whereby leading families or clans presumably occupied large regional centers from where they dominated subordinate groups that inhabited smaller sites – we would expect clearer linkages between both kinds of fortified site.

Early Iron Age (HA D) Hillforts

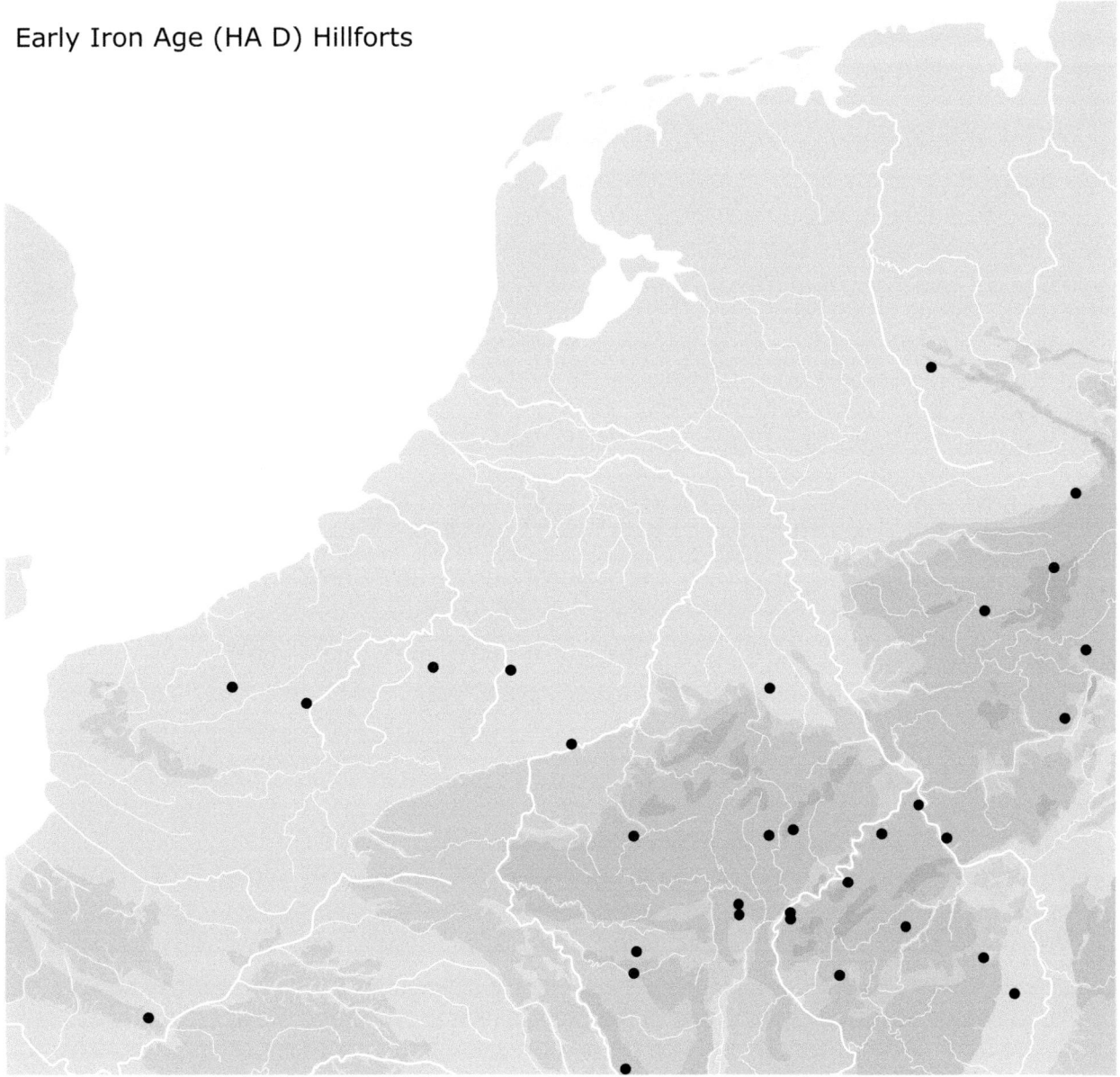

Figure 2: Distribution of newly constructed HA D hillforts[5]

---

[4] Fernández-Götz (2014c: 109-111) lists Bleidenberg, Donnersberg, Kastel-Staadt, Martberg, Otzenhausen, Titelberg, and Wallendorf as examples of this type of large LIA settlement.
[5] Information on hillforts in the study area has been compiled from data found in Collis (1975), Diepeveen-Jansen (2001), Roymans (1990), Sicherl (2007), and Verhoeven (2008). Further data was collected from the oppida.org website, a Culture 2000 program of the European Commission. Last accessed 15 March 2019.

Middle Iron Age (LT A) Hillforts

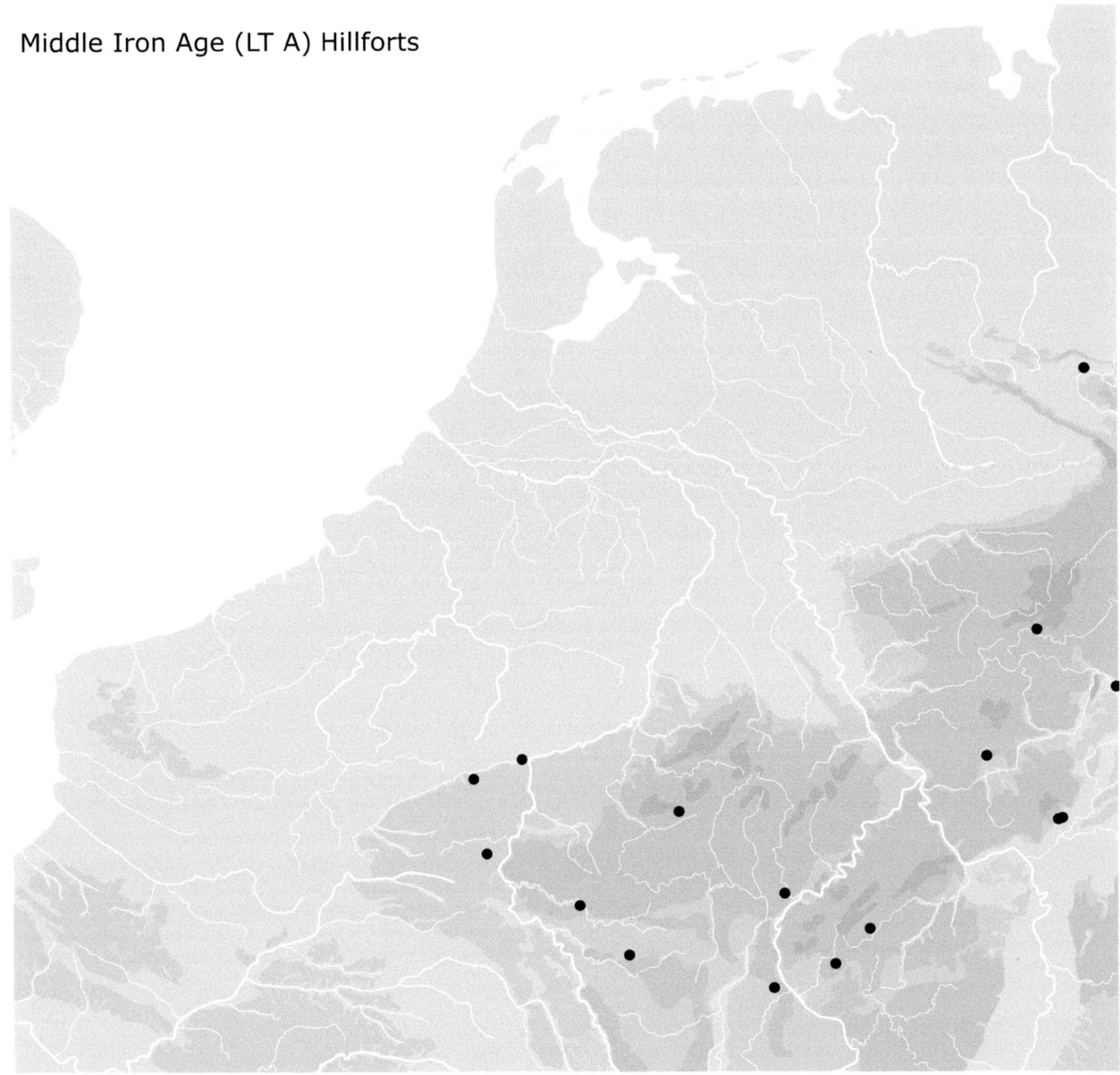

Figure 3: Distribution of newly constructed LT A hillforts

In addition to these large hillforts of the Rhine-Moselle region, a small number of high-lying fortified sites of HA D-LT A date are known from the Belgian Scheldt River region.[6] These seem to have been built in locations where they could command river tributaries and confluences. In contrast to many of the smaller Rhine-Moselle refuges, then, isolation does not appear to have been an important consideration for the occupants of these fortified sites. This is also suggested by the presence of materials like Attic Black glaze ware and imitations of Greek and Etruscan pottery that point to participation in exchange networks extending as far as Central Europe and the Mediterranean World. The occurrence of a locally manufactured red-painted ware (Kemmelberg pottery) at several of these sites also demonstrates participation in regional networks. Together with evidence for chariots and horse gear, these finds have led archaeologists to characterize the fortified settlements of the Scheldt River region as the regional

---

[6] Such as at present-day Kemmelberg, Kesselberg, Kester, and Kooigem (de Mulder and Bourgeois 2011).

Middle Iron Age (LT B) Hillforts

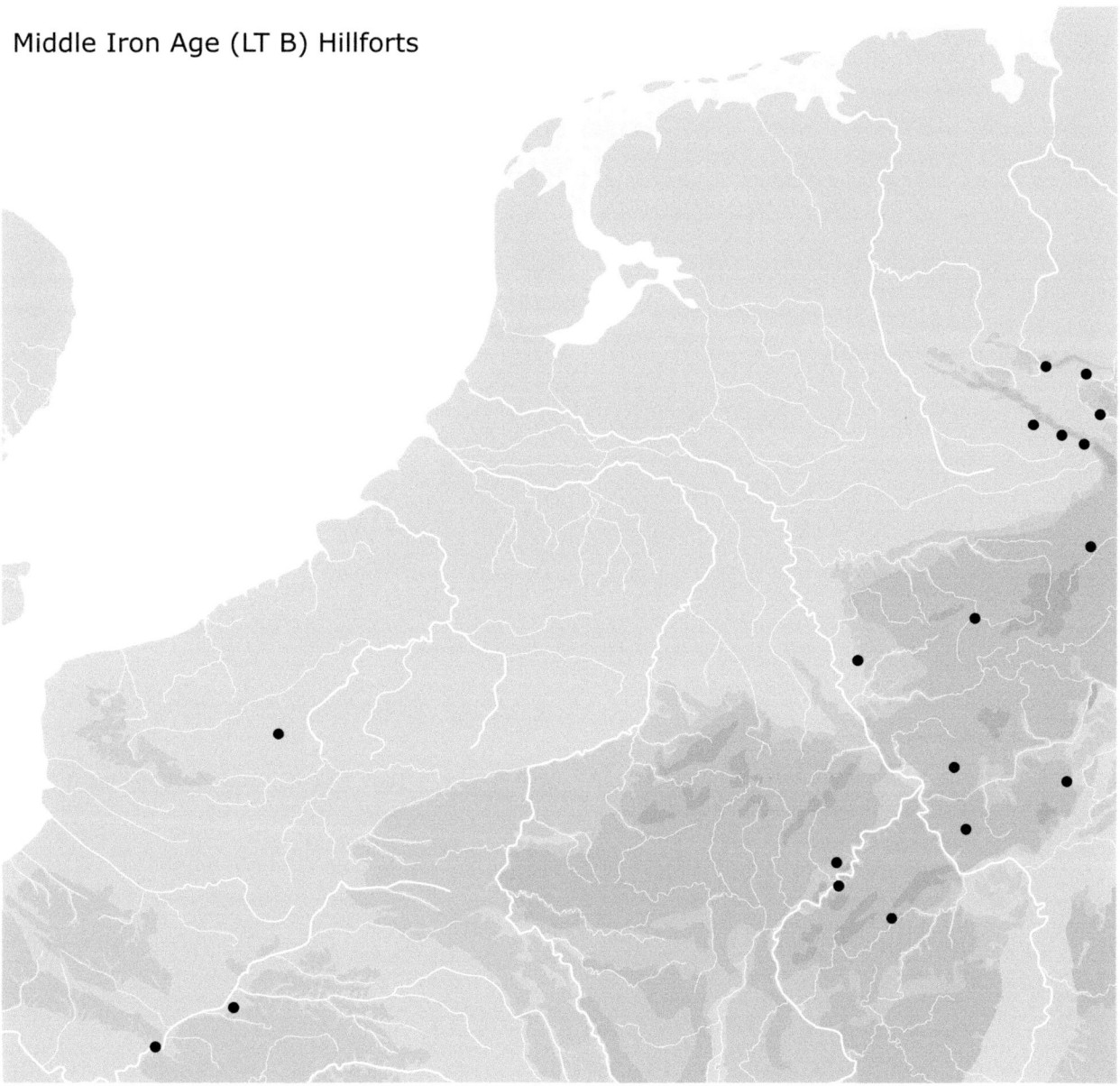

Figure 4: Distribution of newly constructed LT B hillforts

centers of local elites, and are thus deemed comparable to the large hillforts of the Rhine-Moselle region, or even the contemporary princely hillforts of the West-Central Hallstatt world. However, because archaeologists have yet to make a convincing case for significant social stratification within what broadly remained a segmentary society, this notion of indigenous elites gaining social prominence – presumably by controlling the productive output of self-sufficient farming families or the distribution of exotic prestige goods – remains problematic for the northern part of the study area. Notably, the erection of these fortified sites in the Scheldt River region occurred during a time when there was a peak in refuge construction in the wider study area, with the majority of HA D refuges built in the Rhine-Moselle region. For this same period, mortuary evidence points to expansive processes in the Aisne-Marne and Rhine-Moselle regions but contraction in the Scheldt-Meuse region (Mata 2017b: 180). The development of elite centers in the Scheldt river region at a time of demographic and economic decline presents a paradox, then, making it difficult to interpret the attested patterns in terms of social

Late Iron Age (LT C) Hillforts

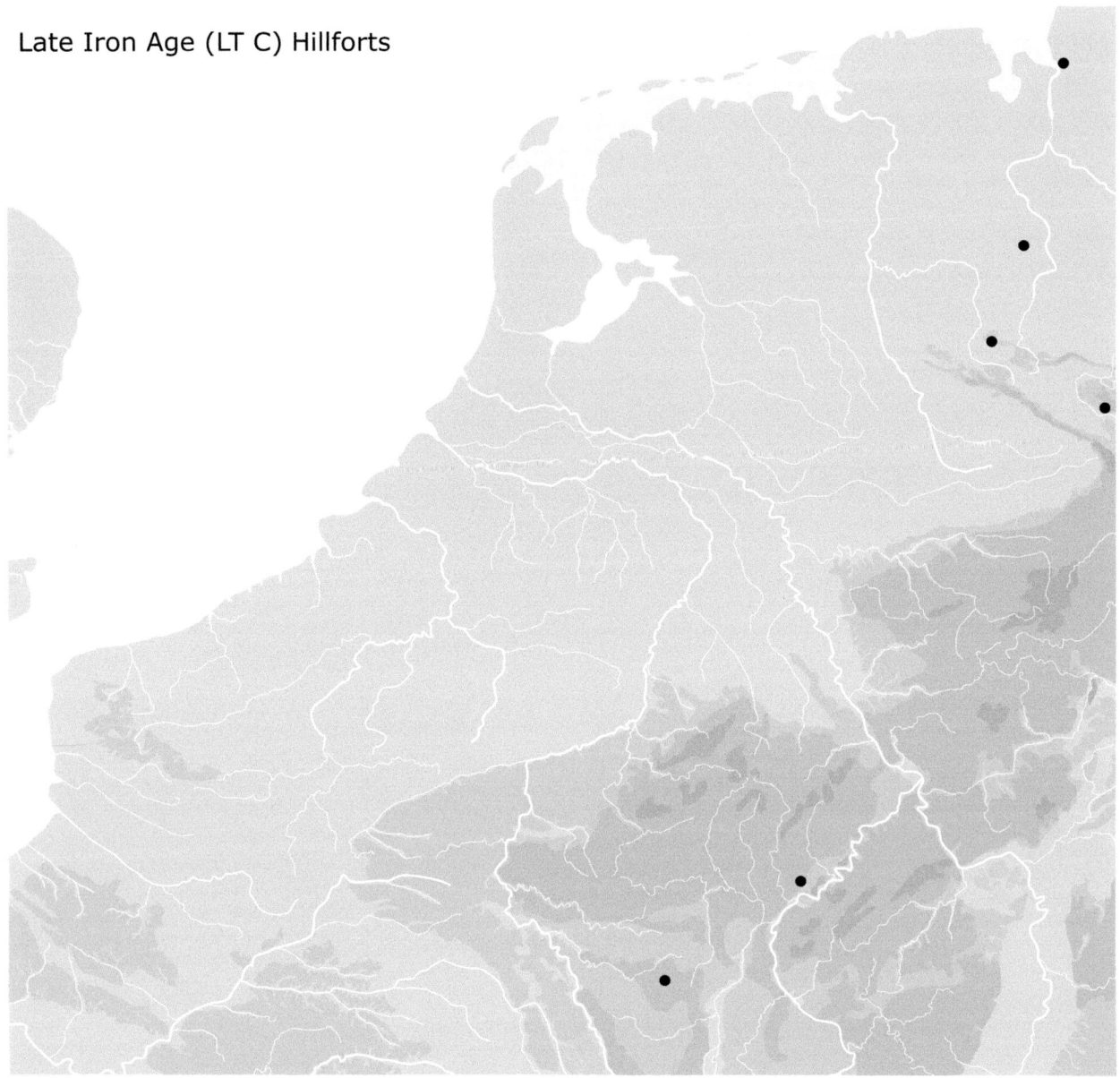

Figure 5: Distribution of newly constructed LT C hillforts

complexification. Instead, the defended sites of the Belgian Scheldt River region are better understood as anomalous manifestations, insertions even, in a normative socio-cultural context.

We can pursue this proposition further by considering the evidence from a small number of exceptionally wealthy 'chieftain's graves' of LHa date that have been found in the same region (Bloemers 1986; Fokkens *et al.* 2012; Fontijn and Fokkens 2007; Roymans 2009; van der Vaart-Verschoof 2017; de Wit 1997/1998).[7] The dominant viewpoint is that these are the resting place of local elites who participated in long-range networks of interaction that spanned West-Central Europe, and through which norms of behavior

---

[7] Locations where LHa 'chiefly burials' have been found in the Scheldt-Meuse region include Court-St.-Etienne, Ede-Bennekom, Haps, Horst-Hegelsom, Meerlo, Oss-Vorstengraf, Oss-Zevenbergen, Rhenen-Koerheuvel, Someren, Uden-Slabroek, and Wijchen, (Bourgeois and van der Vaart-Verschoof 2017: 307; van der Vaart-Verschoof and Schumann 2017: 14).

Late Iron Age (LT D) Hillforts

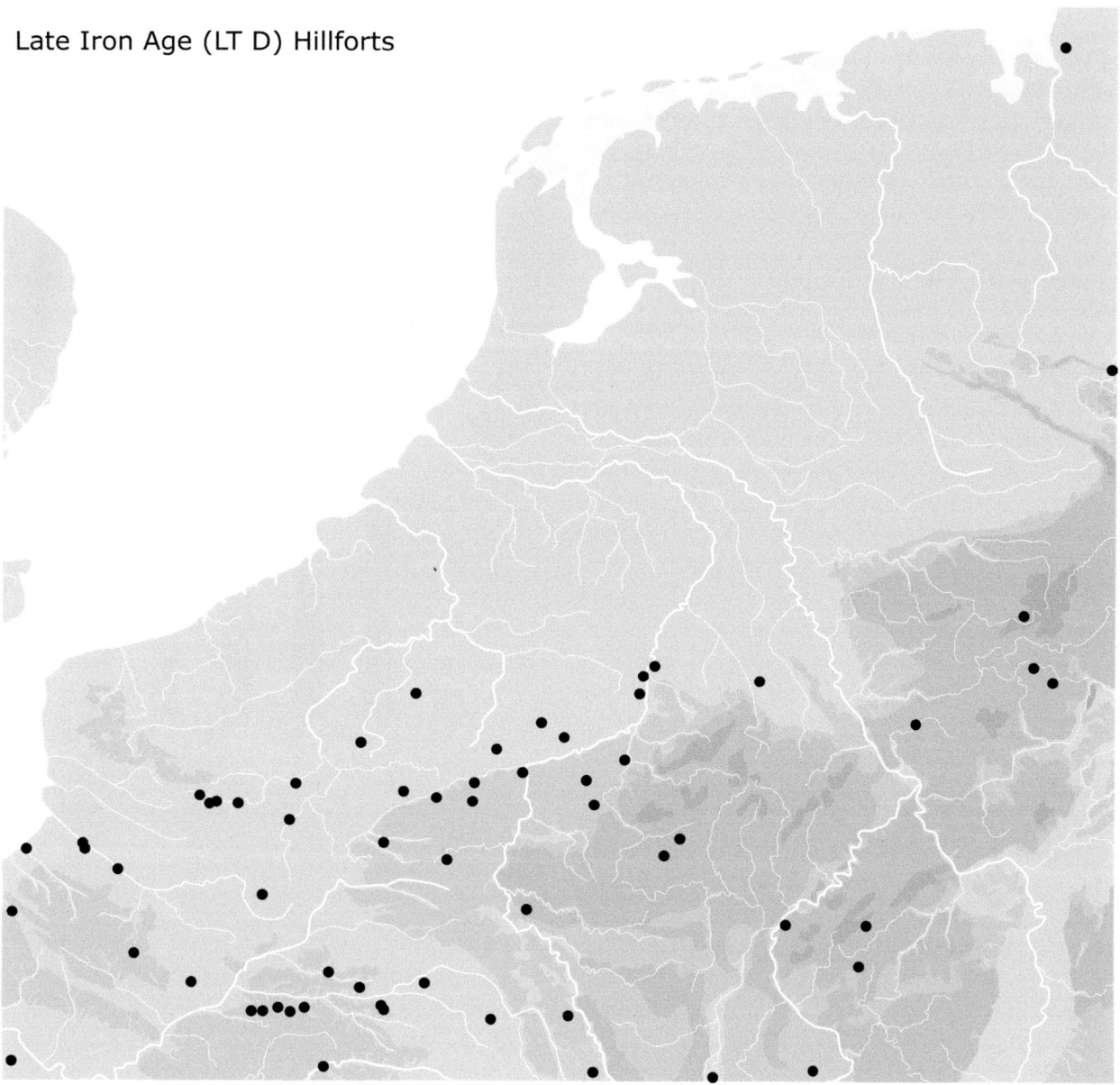

Figure 6: Distribution of newly constructed LT D hillforts

(like burial practices) were shared. Despite the lavishness of these Ha C-D burials, interpretations that suggest the rise of local elites are difficult to maintain when other evidence is considered (e.g. settlement system, economic strategy, technological complexity).[8] Much like the fortified sites of the Scheldt River region, then, these 'chiefly burials' are aberrant within a broadly egalitarian society in which expressions of social differentiation were highly constrained in most spheres of life (de Mulder and Bourgeois 2011: 310). What they show, at most, is that the burial treatment of a small number of individuals during the EIA diverged significantly from normative mortuary rituals that aligned more suitably with socio-economic realities and related cultural ideals.

---

[8] Material wealth cannot uncritically be linked to social rank because it can also point to economic focus (commerce or industry) or materialist ideals. The discovery of skeletal remains of wealthy Hallstatt 'elites' with physical signs of hard labor likewise demonstrates the need for caution (Pope and Ralston 2011: 376).

Notably, the chiefly burials of the northern part of the study area are broadly contemporaneous with LHa *Fürstengräber* found in Central Europe (van der Vaart-Verschoof 2017: 47), and the provenance of certain grave goods also demonstrates linkages with that region. Among them are a type of horse gear that predominantly occurs east of the Rhine (Egg 2017: 60); the only examples found west of the Rhine derive from the chiefly burials of the Scheldt-Meuse region. The evidence for textiles likewise suggests links with Central Europe. Several regions where distinct cloth types were dominant during Ha D - LT A are known (Jørgensen 1992: 124), and Central Europe features uniquely as the most heterogeneous area where several styles occur.[9] Suggestively, it is the Oss type that has been found in widely dispersed locations, including the Netherlands (Oss), Austria (Dürrnberg), Germany (Sonnenberg), and England (Burton Fleming). It strikes me as sensible, then, to reassess the prevailing nativist perspective of limited connectivity between inward-oriented Iron Age communities experiencing universal processes of complexification.[10] Instead, chiefly burials in this part of the study area were likely erected by groups for whom mobility was an important part of lived experience, to the degree that it shaped cultural ideals and ritual practices. Sumptuous burials in which vehicles and horse gear were deposited could be interpreted, then,

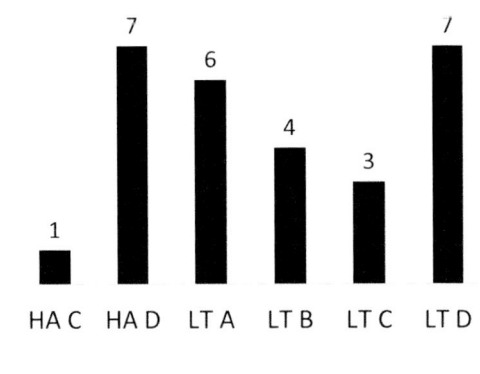

Figure 7: Number of newly constructed hillforts and scale diversity per period[11]

not as the final resting place of sedentary rulers of local farming communities who maintained limited long-distance connections,[12] but instead of members of mobile groups that combined pastoralism and horsemanship with specialist craftsmanship and trading. As I will argue below, it is highly likely that these itinerant groups regularly entered Northwest Europe in pursuit of a distinct resource, namely human captives.

In an effort to examine Iron Age transformations without accepting the inevitability of social complexification, or relying on reifying identifiers like 'barbarian' or 'warrior', it is necessary to try

---

[9] The Huldremose type is mainly found in Scandinavian regions, north of Jutland. The Haraldskjaer type is predominantly found distributed throughout the North European Lowlands, broadly corresponding with the Jastorf cultural sphere. The La Joya type is encountered in the Iberian Peninsula. Lastly, four types (Döhren, Dürrnberg, Oss, and Vače) are encountered across West-Central Europe.

[10] That such reconsideration is warranted is also increasingly becoming apparent from chemical analyses of human skeletal remains that are demonstrating that Iron Age mobility and interaction were in fact substantial (van den Broeke 2014: 17; Oelze 2012; Oelze et al. 2012; Scheeres 2014: 4; Scheeres et al. 2013).

[11] The sample contains 142 hillfort sites. To measure scale diversity, each hillforts was allocated to one of seven arbitrary scales: 1-10, 11-20, 21-30, 31-40, 41-50, 50-100, and 100-250 ha (Mata 2017b: 227).

[12] While the mortuary ceremonies of such groups could be impressive, it is worth emphasizing that even the larger of these sumptuous burial mounds (e.g. Oss) was only three meters high. This level of monumentality may not have been impressive enough to have functioned as significant loci of communal memory, commemoration, or outward display (Gerritsen 2003: 194).

and determine what kind of historical factors shaped patterns in refuge construction, and to consider the forces that caused martiality to receive such emphasis in the ideological systems of countless Iron Age communities. To understand these regional particularities better, we can begin by considering the spatial distribution of refuges. Figures 2-6 not only reflect the number of newly built refuges per period, they show where in the study area they were built. During the latter half of the EIA (Ha D), the majority are found in the eastern half of the study area, primarily the Rhine-Moselle region. The situation is reversed during the latter half of the LIA (LT D) when most are found in the western half of the study area centered on the Aisne-Marne region. If it can be accepted that security and interaction were closely linked, then variability in connectivity could possibly explain geographic differences in refuge construction. It is important, however, to distinguish between connectivity understood in terms of a geographic allowance for mobility and interaction (how a landscape facilitates or constrains movement and communication), and in terms of socio-historical dynamics (who interacted, when, how, and to what end). Both points merit brief elaboration.

In order to gain access to Mediterranean consumers and producers, Celto-Germanic traders in Northwest Europe could use two important passage routes. West of the Alps, the Rhône River provided direct access to the Western Mediterranean region. Using short overland routes, several major river systems of Northwest Europe (Loire, Seine, Meuse, and Rhine) could be used to access the Saône-Rhône system. North of the Alps, the Danube river system linked northern rivers (Rhine, Weser, Elbe, Oder, and Vistula) with Adriatic and Pontic trade systems. It is clear, then, that the communities of the Rhine-Moselle region were ideally positioned to link to western (Seine and Meuse), northern (Rhine and Weser), southern (Saône-Rhône), and eastern (Danube) exchange routes. Aisne-Marne groups were less ideally situated, with the greatest potential for extra-regional connectivity provided by Seine and Meuse routes. The fact that refuges do not occur here in any significant numbers until LT D perhaps speaks to this lower potential for extra-regional connectivity, and the same could be said for communities situated in the Scheldt-Meuse region. Indeed, the distribution of Mediterranean imports in the study area suggests this as well; the earliest arrival (Ha D) of Etruscan bronze wares occurred in the Rhine-Moselle region, when these remained absent elsewhere in the study area. This changed during LT A-B when such imports were also deposited in the Aisne-Marne region, though in limited quantities; it is not until the LIA that imports (e.g. Italic Campanian ware and South Gallic wine amphorae) were deposited in substantial quantities there. This contrasts sharply with the Scheldt-Meuse region where Mediterranean imports never occurred in appreciable numbers. But, as noted, it is important to distinguish between a potential for connectivity and actual interaction. One need only consider how the low-lying coastal and riverine landscapes of the Scheldt-Meuse region offered a high potential for connectivity. Indeed, this would become a crucial factor in the later establishment of the Roman Rhine frontier. Yet, this apparently did not encourage significant social complexification among the segmentary communities that inhabited these areas during the Iron Age. Moreover, while the shifting engagement of Aisne-Marne and Rhine-Moselle groups in extra-regional networks is noteworthy, this clearly did not result from any changes in the geographic conditions that facilitated or constrained connectivity. In other words, it is necessary to consider the socio-historical dynamics of exchange systems.

From the investigation of burial assemblages in the study area it has long been clear that a wide range of tradable goods made of non-local materials (e.g. Baltic amber, Atlantic tin, Atlantic or Mediterranean coral, and Mediterranean glass and bronze) circulated throughout Northwest Europe during the long Iron Age. But, what goods or materials were exchanged for Mediterranean imports specifically? While Roman literary sources of Late Republican and Early Imperial date occasionally mention trade goods that moved through European exchange systems, I will proceed from the assumption that it was not agricultural products that encouraged Mediterranean traders to tap into Late Hallstatt and La Tène trade circuits (Kindstedt 2012: 105). Indeed, there were few things that could be imported from Northwest

Europe that were not also available from nearer sources (Dietler 1989: 129). Rather, the greatest interest was for metals and special commodities like amber and furs for which there existed fluctuating but enduring demand in the Mediterranean region because sources there were scarce or absent (King 1990: 120; Kristiansen 1998: 180). Sources of metal ore are relatively rare in the study area, though gold and iron deposits may have been exploited by Rhine-Moselle groups inhabiting the German Hunsrück area during LT A (Morteani and Northover 1995: 124; Shefton 1995: 11). The distribution of tin sources along the Atlantic Rim (mainly Brittany and Cornwall) attracted Mediterranean attention from a very early date, with the rivers Garonne, Loire, and possibly the Seine functioning as important transport routes (Giumlia-Mair and Lo Schiavo 2003). The study area lacks tin deposits, however, such that there was no reason for merchants to venture there for that particular resource. Amber, by contrast, has a far better potential for having been exchanged by local groups for Mediterranean goods. The vast majority of amber circulating in prehistoric Europe derived from North Sea and Baltic sources from where it was transported south via Rhine, Weser, Elbe, Oder, and Vistula river routes. For Western Mediterranean consumers, amber likely moved through the Saône-Rhône corridor, or along an eastern Alpine route to the Adriatic and beyond (Angelini and Bellintani 2005; Czebreszuk 2003, 2007).[13] Furs brought from boreal regions will have moved along these same 'Amber Roads'. Within the study area, the Rhine likely was the main route along which such northern resources were transported to southern markets, which again shows how Rhine-Moselle communities were better positioned compared to their neighbors of the Aisne-Marne and Scheldt-Meuse regions. When considering the commercial potential of the study area, then, amber and furs derived from northern European sources seemingly had the greatest potential for drawing the attention of southern merchants, and, consequently, for drawing Celto-Germanic communities into 'global' trade circuits. Yet, it remains difficult to see how amber- and fur-trading could have impacted shifting levels of insecurity (as suggested by patterns in refuge construction) or encourage the well-attested cultural significance of martiality (as shown by the widespread deposition of weaponry, armor, horse gear, and chariots in sacred and mortuary contexts). A way forward starts with the recognition that local and regional trends did not manifest in isolation from broader ('global') historical developments (Mata 2017a), and this urges a closer consideration of events and processes occurring in the Mediterranean region. Not because of some uncritical admiration of Greek, Etruscan, or Roman cultural achievements, but because of a pragmatic consideration of historical realities.

---

[13] Amber-trading groups like the Vindelici and Veneti seemed to have monopolized East Alpine trade routes during the LIA (Pliny the Elder *Natural History* 37, 43). Taking control of Aquileia situated at the head of the Adriatic (*c.* 180 BC) allowed Rome to dominate the flow of amber into the Italic peninsula and beyond. Despite the formation of the Danubian frontier, the role of Aquileia as importer of raw and exporter of carved amber continued until *c.* AD 180 when frequent wars with trans-Danubian groups finally cut off Central European supply routes. By this time, however, another important center for the amber trade had arisen on the Rhine at Cologne, where workshops operated from the second to the fourth century A.D. (Veldman 2003: 34).

Historicizing Regional Dynamics

We can start by considering the two hard to ignore temporal peaks in refuge construction, the first around the end of the EIA (Ha D), the other during the second half of the LIA (LT D).[1] What was transpiring in the Mediterranean world during these periods, and how did this shape interactions with the peoples of Northwest Europe? The Ha D period lasted a little over a century, from c. 600 to 475 BC. Significant for this period is the founding of Greek trading entrepôts in southern France, most notably Massalia (Marseille) around 600 BC.[2] Equally noteworthy are the political alliances between Etruscan city-states that formed in response to growing Greek and Carthaginian influence in the Western Mediterranean. This also encouraged Etruscan colonization of the Po valley in northern Italy, and the establishment of emporia in the northern Adriatic region. These developments had important consequences for trans-Alpine relations. It is in this period that we witness the rise of princely hillforts and the interment of 'indigenous elites' in sumptuous burials containing vehicles, weaponry, fine wares, precious metals, and Greek and Etruscan imports throughout the West-Central Hallstatt world.

In order to understand better the nature and scale of trading between Mediterranean and trans-Alpine communities, it is useful to start by considering the temporal and geographic distribution of Mediterranean wine amphorae during the latter part of the EIA (Sacchetti 2016). The earliest of these arrived during the second half of the sixth century BC and are found at princely residences in eastern France (Burgundy and Franche-Comté) and southwestern Germany (Baden-Württemberg). In a subsequent phase (late sixth-early fifth century BC), amphorae are found more widely in these two regions. The first peak in refuge construction in the study area occurred during these two phases; most notably in the Rhine-Moselle region where the earliest Mediterranean imports (bronze vessels) are found. Subsequently, amphorae are solely found in France during the first half of the fifth century BC, concentrating around the Saône-Rhône corridor.[3] Lastly, a fourth phase dates to the second half of the fifth century when the circulation of Mediterranean amphorae in France was again more widespread. During this ELT phase we witness a stronger focus on kinship and social differentiation in the Aisne-Marne and Rhine-Moselle regions (Mata 2017b: 211), developments likely encouraged by increased involvement in supra-regional exchange networks.

It has to be emphasized, however, that the quantity of Mediterranean wine amphorae circulating through Northwest Europe was generally quite low, with distributions also remaining rather insular geographically.[4] Furthermore, most sites where wine amphorae have been found can be allocated solely to one of the four phases described above. What the spatio-temporal distribution of wine amphorae across the West-Central Hallstatt world points to, then, is the highly intermittent and confined materialization

---

[1] Depending on the scholar's perspective, these peaks might be considered high or low points in socio-cultural development. When considering the transformative impact of insecurity and anxiety it is difficult to argue in positive terms (e.g. Pope and Ralston 2011: 387) that HA D and LT D represent periods of societal improvement or cultural effervescence.

[2] Fernández-Götz and Arnold (2017: 186) are right to note that processes of differentiation already manifested during Ha C, prior to the construction of 'princely' hillforts during Ha D. However, just because indigenous Ha C developments cannot be related directly to the later Ha D foundation of Greek colonies in southern France does not mean that they manifested in isolation. It simply means archaeologists have yet to figure out why these transitions occurred when they did, and through what local-global dynamics.

[3] This probably does not reflect a waning of Etruscan participation in trans-Alpine trading, merely that wine amphorae were primarily moved through southern France at this time. Etruscan merchants may have focused more on the trade in bronze wares that would come to inspire La Tène stylistic innovations.

[4] That trade was both intermittent and directional (i.e. potential trade partners were consciously targeted) is perhaps also suggested by the distribution of Italic bronze wares in the Rhine-Moselle region in the ELT period. Bronze *situlae* from northern Italy show an eastern distribution, while beaked flagons are somewhat later more dominant towards the West (Fernández-Götz 2014c: 87).

of trans-local engagements. These are not signs of a gradual and steady process of complexification driven by elite differentiation and facilitated by resource control. Rather, what we are seeing are incidental and temporary engagements between local individuals (and their kin) and non-local actors (most likely traders of Mediterranean origin or indigenous intermediaries) becoming archaeologically visible. Whatever it was that motivated Greek or Etruscan merchants to establish relations with LHa and ELT indigenous groups, this was successfully facilitated by shared norms of hospitality and reciprocity, with a central role attributable to wine consumption. Indeed, the high appreciation of wine made it ideal for limited gift exchange and treaty trade (Sacchetti 2016: 261). It is highly likely that some groups situated in the study area primarily exchanged human captives for Mediterranean luxury goods.

While the contemporaneity of Mediterranean and trans-Alpine developments has long been thought significant (Rowlands et al. 1987), and the importance of indigenous valuations of non-local products certainly cannot be ignored (Dietler 1990), it has to be asked why Greek mercantile activity expanded into the Western Mediterranean region when it did.[5] While oft-considered variables like demographic growth and resource demand may certainly have been important drivers (Wells 2002: 361), particular socio-political developments taking place in Greece around this time strike me as more pertinent. Illustrative of this are the radical political reforms promoted by the Athenian statesman Solon (c. 594 BC) that resulted in the emancipation of debt slaves and the protection of the poor from enslavement by fellow citizens. Solon's efforts also led to a significant expansion of commercial enterprise, the goal of which seems to have been to transform an agrarian city-state into a mercantile powerhouse. Crucially, the emancipation of debt-slaves and proscription of citizen enslavement resulted in acute labor shortages, and this encouraged a significant expansion of slave trading. Moreover, these processes did not solely take place in Athens. Other Greek city-states experienced similar developments around the same time (Robinson 2008). It is not unreasonable to argue, then, that increased labor demands, investment in commerce, and a number of other related factors (Finley 1959; Miller 2008: 75; Scheidel 2008:118) resulted in a significant expansion of the Greek slave trade, and, together, they drove the expansion of mercantile colonialism in the Black Sea region and the Western Mediterranean. This is not to say that forced servitude was not an important part of the Greek experience before that time (Patterson 2008, 65). It certainly was. However, it is equally true that a number of distinct developments led to an increase in the socio-economic importance of chattel slavery in the Classical Greek world.[6] This had clear repercussions for the peoples of temperate Europe.[7]

---

[5] The pessimistic notion that Mediterranean traders were largely ignorant of the origins of certain goods like tin (e.g. Dietler 2010: 104) strikes me as unwarranted. The clear ignorance displayed by some Greco-Roman philosophers or poets merely shows that worldly knowledge was not held by everyone. See my discussion on the historical manifestation of trans-cultural formations (Mata 2017a: 14).

[6] The Greek philosopher Aristotle offers a glimpse of related attitudes and ideals: 'Of property, the first and most indispensable kind is that which is also best and most amenable to housecraft; and this is the human chattel. Our first step therefore must be to procure good slaves' (*Economics* 1.1344a). The Greek historian Polybius, in similar vein, writes: 'For those commodities which are the first necessaries of existence, cattle and slaves, are confessedly supplied by the districts round the Pontus in greater profusion, and of better quality, than by any others' (*Histories* 4.38).

[7] Often referenced for his pioneering work on Greek slavery, Finley (1959, 1962, and 1980) has argued that the incidental and opportunistic exploitation of human labor in prehistoric times gradually transformed into a socially institutionalized and economically formalized phenomenon. Tchernia (1983: 99) mentions how Greeks in Thrace, and Romans in Gaul, were not primarily interested in expanding commerce in salt and wine but were actively working to expand the slave trade. Braund and Tsetskhladze (1989) have looked at the slave trade in the Black Sea region, in particular the export of slaves from Colchis to the Achaean. Rosivach (1999) has written about the ideological aspects of the Greek slave system, while Gavriljuk (2003) more recently examined the Greco-Scythian slave trade of the 6th-5th centuries BC. Bodel (2005) offers a study of Roman slave traders who commonly contributed to an illicit trade in abducted provincial citizens. Lewis (2011 and 2015) has looked at the Classical Greek slave trade with Persian territories and emphasized its considerable proportions. There is, in fact, much interest for issues of scale in the literature on Greek and Roman slavery, yet many remain skeptical of the high numbers communicated by the ancient sources. To illustrate, the Greek rhetorician Atheneus provides census figures that suggest that a mere seven per cent of the population of Attica in the later fourth century BC was not enslaved (Taylor 2001: 29).

Slavery also became a common feature of Early Etruscan (Ha C-D) society, where households commonly used domestic slaves to perform everyday tasks (Benelli 2013; Nash-Briggs 2002, 2003). Slaves with certain appealing qualities, like light skin and hair, seem to have been highly valued by differentiating elites interested in flaunting possession of physically attractive women and youths. Their inevitable replacement ensured a constant demand, and there is little to doubt their northern European origin. While Italic and Celto-Germanic peoples had undoubtedly long maintained close relations by exchanging goods, people, and knowledge, this situation likely changed from the EIA (Ha C) onwards when Etruscan society became increasingly stratified (Dietler 2010: 102). The socio-economic importance of slaves only increased when Etruscan cities founded new colonies in the Po Valley and the Adriatic region. There, wealth accumulation led to growing competition and inequality, ultimately causing a 'crisis of the Etruscan serfdom' (Torelli 2000: 203). It is highly likely that these socio-historical developments resulted in an expansion of Etruscan slave trading in trans-Alpine Europe.

From this I conclude that the LHa increase in refuge construction in the study area can best be understood as having resulted from an expansion of slaver activity throughout trans-Alpine Europe, and this was a development that can be linked directly to a growing demand for exploitable human bodies in the Mediterranean world. If this proposition can be accepted, then subsequent patterns in refuge construction can likewise be understood better when they are related to long-term fluctuations in the 'international' slave trade. During LT A-C, we witness a gradual decline in refuge construction in the study area, with a lowest number built during LT C. This is a period that archaeologists and art historians have long associated with a pronounced degree of stylistic experimentation visible in the material culture of groups situated on the northwestern periphery of the Hallstatt world. Over the course of the MIA, the La Tène 'aesthetic phenomenon' gradually extended across temperate Europe, from the Atlantic to the Pontic (Brun 1994; Cunliffe 1997; Wells 2002).[8] This development coincided with the abandonment of most LHa 'princely' hillforts, sites formerly occupied by those with the highest likelihood of having been involved in a slave trade. With little evidence for larger village-like agglomerations during subsequent periods, it seems that people throughout West-Central Europe predominantly came to occupy small unenclosed settlements, a development that perhaps points to more secure conditions. Some have argued that social differentiation did become more widespread at this time, a process that Pope and Ralston put in terms of wider 'access to status display' (2011: 388). Communities may also have become better organized militarily because warrior burials became a common feature, and weaponry was increasingly deposited outside sacred and mortuary contexts. It is from written sources, furthermore, that we know of trans-Alpine tribal confederacies settling in northern Italy and partaking in Romano-Etruscan conflicts, and of Gallic mercenaries serving Hellenistic rulers and 'migrating' considerable distances to settle in faraway territories (Arnold and Murray 2002). Thus, for Celto-Germanic groups across West-Central Europe, the MIA can broadly be characterized as one of growing cultural confidence, political-economic initiative, and military assertiveness (Lejars 2012). In the study area, we see a contemporary decline in refuge construction in the South, and increased locational stability (i.e. farmsteads lasting multiple generations) and settlement nucleation in the North (de Hingh 2000: 37). The first half of the ELT period, in particular, provides signs for increased material wealth, higher levels of security, interest for technological innovation and stylistic experimentation, and a greater willingness to engage a wider world.

---

[8] Rhine-Moselle groups seem to have been closely associated with the earliest stylistic innovations in La Tène material culture believed to have been inspired by Etruscan forms. Slaving in West-Central Europe undoubtedly played a significant role in the rise and spread of artistic styles and symbolic repertoires, just like 'the transmission of eastern characteristics to European art' seems to have been affected by the Greek slave trade (Guler 2013: 21). Also see Cameron (2008 and 2011) and Lenski (2008) on the capacity of slaves to affect cultural change.

If it can be accepted that slaving expanded in the LHa period, then the subsequent developments described above might be related to a relative drop in the scale and frequency of such activity.[9] It probably is no happenstance that the noted decline in refuge construction coincided with a decrease in the occurrence of Greek pottery in trans-Alpine Europe (Walsh 2014), a concurrence that can perhaps best be understood in reference to the geo-political situation in the Greek East. Between c. 500-450 BC, conflicts between the Persian Empire and various Greek city-states greatly affected Mediterranean exchange systems, including the flow of slaves (Lewis 2011). This situation hardly improved in subsequent decades, when numerous city-states competed with each other politically and economically. Between c. 430-400 BC, protracted warfare resulted in the death and enslavement of countless men, women, and children, and widespread devastation of land and settlements (Kagan 2003). While it remains difficult to assess the impact of Eastern Mediterranean events on mercantile activity across West-Central Europe, Greek entrepôts in the Western Mediterranean will undoubtedly have had great difficulty continuing business as usual with indigenous groups when goods like wine and fine wares had to be imported from eastern suppliers. It is likely that the commencement of Massalian colonial enterprise (i.e. the foundation or annexation of trade emporia by Massalia) was a consequence of a long-term disruption of trans-Mediterranean commerce. Etruscan communities undoubtedly responded to this new Massalian assertiveness by strengthening their control over Alpine trade routes.[10] Indeed, relations between Etruscan and trans-Alpine actors likely were quite strong. Literary sources show how Etruscan city-states used political alliances with Celtic groups to deal with competitors in Italy, most notably Rome (Nash-Briggs 2003: 257). Gradually, though, the privileged position of Etruscan cities diminished due to the expansion of Roman power, and this was a development that Celto-Germanic groups were forced to negotiate as well. As the Romans sought to gain influence over the lucrative trade networks that linked trans-Alpine and Mediterranean communities, they became faced with assertive and confident barbarians who were logistically competent enough to come to the aid of political allies and settle in distant but undoubtedly familiar lands.

In the study area, the highest temporal peak in refuge construction is a strong indicator for changing conditions during the LIA. In contrast to the predominantly eastern distribution of HA D refuges, most LT D refuges are found to the west in the Aisne-Marne region. There, archaeologists have noticed a contemporary abandonment of farmsteads and occupation of large defended settlements (Haselgrove 2007). Similar large-scale settlements are also encountered in the Rhine-Moselle region, where earlier (LT A) hilltop sites were regularly re-occupied (Fernández-Götz 2014c: 144). Mortuary contexts also show clear signs of greater wealth disparity (e.g. import of luxury goods, substantial grave good deposition, and grave monumentality), reflecting a desire among local family groups to differentiate themselves within the community. In this same period, the expression of martial ideology is no longer restricted to mortuary contexts but also occurred in everyday and religious contexts, perhaps pointing to a militarization of society. Yet, these developments had started before LT D, when LT B-C trends of contraction and decline in the study area (Mata 2017b: 191) coincided with a Roman consolidation of power in the Italic peninsula (c. 280 BC). This not only affected the trade relations of Etruscans and their trans-Alpine partners, it gradually reconfigured a broader political-economic system in which Celto-Germanic groups had a vested interest. That it was exactly

---

[9] Like all commercial enterprise, slave trading will have been affected by inevitable shifts in supply and demand. While numerous factors were at play, there is little doubt that an increase in military conflicts throughout the Mediterranean basin will have impacted the Celto-Germanic slave trade; when each military triumph could enslave tens of thousands individuals, the marketability of imported slaves was increasingly uncertain. At the same time, the interest for specialty slaves – like women and children with particular aesthetic qualities – will have persisted.

[10] The attested 'shift in trade from Greek Massalia to Etruscan Spina around 400 BC' (Arnold and Murray 2002: 113) is indicative of these developments. That cross-Alpine trade continued is shown, for example, by the enduring presence of bronze wares in Rhine-Moselle burials.

in the subsequent LT D period that a zone of large defended settlements (*oppida*) formed across West-Central Europe (Collis 1984; Wells 2002; Woolf 1993) was no historical happenstance, then, but instead points to a transformation of political-economic realities in general, and to increased Roman assertiveness in particular (Wells 2005: 56).[11] The expansion of Roman hegemony throughout the Western Mediterranean transformed relations with trans-Alpine Europe significantly, with major consequences for communities in the study area.

Socio-historical developments unfolding in Roman Italy (Hopkins 1978; Jongman 2003) strongly suggest that it again was increased slaving activity specifically that impacted populations throughout Northwest Europe during the LIA. Like their Greek and Etruscan counterparts, citizens of the Roman Republic had long clashed with political leadership for economic opportunities and legal protections. Such appeals occasionally received legislative attention, for example, when Roman debt bondage (*nexum*) was abolished in 326 BC (Finley 1980; Kleijwegt 2013). Yet, because agricultural land continued to concentrate in the hands of wealthy elites, ever larger numbers of peasants were driven into dispossessed poverty (Cunliffe 1997; Harris 2011). This situation was compounded by a growing use of slaves in agriculture, manufacturing, and service economies, which significantly reduced small-holder competitiveness and labor employment among free citizens (Lenski 2008: 82; Miller 2008: 79; Scheidel 2008: 115). These trends caused a substantial demographic shift to towns and cities where the impoverished masses became a source of civic unrest and social instability. Attempts to push through land reforms – most famously by Tiberius Gracchus (133 BC) and his brother Gaius Gracchus (123 BC)[12] – largely failed due to the unwillingness of politically dominant landowners to redistribute wealth. Moreover, they combined this reluctance with a readiness to remedy societal problems through expansionist endeavors. This had radical consequences for Rome's engagements with trans-Alpine Europe. Military conflicts, in particular, increased in frequency and impact. One series of conflicts, the Cimbrian Wars (113-101 BC), proved so challenging to Roman military leadership that they triggered significant organizational innovations (the Marian reforms).[13] One notable change was the formation of a standing army of professional soldiers. This was made possible by allowing the landless poor into military service; prior to this change in recruitment policy a land ownership qualification prevented most citizens from joining the ranks. Mass enlistment of the rural and urban poor undoubtedly resulted in further labor shortages throughout the Italic peninsula, at least wherever slaves were not readily at hand. This may indeed have become a common situation following the third Servile War (73-71 BC) when tens of thousands of slaves escaped captivity (Appian *Civil War* 1.116).[14] Roman efforts to suppress seaborne piracy, an important source of slaves, only exacerbated this trend.[15] Thus, Italic labor shortages will have increased substantially over the course of the second and first centuries BC,

---

[11] The fact that Roman mercantile activity across northern Gaul increased significantly (Loughton 2009: 99) following the decline of Arvernian political power in Central Gaul, and the formation of the Roman province of Gallia Narbonensis in 121 BC, is a regional manifestation of this broader geo-political trend.

[12] Plutarch offers revealing commentary: 'But his brother Caius, in a certain pamphlet, has written that as Tiberius was passing through Tuscany on his way to Numantia, and observed the dearth of inhabitants in the country, and that those who tilled its soil or tended its flocks there were imported barbarian slaves, he then first conceived the public policy which was the cause of countless ills to the two brothers. However, the energy and ambition of Tiberius were most of all kindled by the people themselves, who posted writings on porticoes, house-walls, and monuments, calling upon him to recover for the poor the public land' (*Parallel Lives* 8.7).

[13] Diodorus Siculus provides the following intriguing commentary: 'As part of the command of Marius against the Cimbrians, the senate had given him a commission to raise men from the countries beyond the seas; to which end, Marius sent envoys to Nicomedes king of Bithynia, requesting him to send some men as auxiliaries; but Nicomedes replied that most of the Bithynians had been taken away as slaves by the tax-collectors, and were dispersed throughout the province' (*Historical Library* 36.3).

[14] Including countless Gauls and Germans (Caesar *Gallic Wars* I.40; Orosius *History against the Pagans* V.24).

[15] While it is true that the sources for Mediterranean slaves were varied (Harris 1999; Scheidel 1997), two significant sources were largely erased when Roman political and military ascendency reduced the frequency and scale of warfare and piracy around the Mediterranean world.

resulting in a growing demand for slaves and concomitant increase of slaving activity in Northwest Europe.[16]

---

[16] A number of studies support this overall impression. Crawford (1977: 123), for example, uses numismatic data to argue that some 30,000 slaves were removed annually from the lower Danube basin between 60-30 BC. This is adjusted by Taylor (2001: 29) to the incredible number of 300,000. Objections based on carrying capacity arguments are easily countered by the realization that captives were not exclusively extracted from adjacent regions, but were often transported over long distances. For Gaul, Tchernia (1983: 98) suggests that we can expect 15,000 slaves to have been removed annually during the last century of the Roman Republic, culminating in Caesar's incredible number of one million enslaved Gauls. Harris (1999) and Scheidel (1997 and 2011), moreover, have examined the demographics of the Roman slave system, and, despite disagreements about quantities, argue that the Mediterranean demand for slaves, while highly mutable, was enduring and in certain times and places extremely high. Schörle (2012) and Wilson (2012) have examined the Saharan slave trade, both concluding that it was at least as substantial as the medieval trade in slaves (*c.* 3-5000 slaves annually).

Exploring Dimensions of Slaving and Enslavement

So far, I have looked at the evidence for refuge construction in the study area and suggested that spatio-temporal patterns can be understood best by considering certain events and processes unfolding in the Mediterranean world. I will next explore multiple (material, behavioral, and ideological) dimensions of Iron Age slaving and enslavement in order to try and understand the consequences of these distinct historical phenomena for the peoples of Northwest Europe. I first turn to LIA evidence for wine and wine-drinking paraphernalia in trans-Alpine Europe because literary (Polybius *Histories* 4.38; Strabo *Geography* V 1.8, XI 2.3) and iconographic (Bodel 2005: 189; Koester 2008: 774) evidence clearly demonstrates the significance of wine for the slave trade. Curiously, archaeologists have not generally considered this association despite having demonstrated the strong social significance of wine consumption among indigenous groups (Arnold 1999; Braund and Tsetskhladze 1989; Dietler 1990; Loughton 2009; Vencl 1994). That both were closely linked is only occasionally noted (Tchernia 1983). Fentress (2011), for example, shows how large quantities of amphorae are commonly found at enclosed ritual centers of mid second to mid first century BC date, and these are believed to be remains of potlatch-type feasting. Over the course of decades, large amounts of food and drink were consumed periodically at these sites in ritualized ways. It is not difficult to imagine, with Fentress (2011: 65), that such sacred sites were associated with the slave trade. If such a linkage can be accepted, then the earliest manifestation of these 'feasting sanctuaries' suggests an intensification of the slave trade around the end of the third century BC (mid LT C).

This broadly coincides with Rome gaining hegemony in the Italic peninsula, and when a range of new developments (social stratification, militarization, settlement fortification, and communal sanctuaries) started emerging across West-Central Europe (Arnold 2011; Lejars 2012). It is likely that from this time onwards (and after a possible LT B-C respite) Italic slave traders traveled with increased frequency to Gallic trade centers such as Chalon (Saône river), Lyon (Rhône river), and Toulouse (Garonne river) in order to exchange wine for slaves. Because merchants clearly operated under conditions assisted by Roman commercial imperialism (Miller 2008: 71; Tchernia 1983: 99) – whereby high-profit ventures were aggressively pursued with assurances granted by military power – the main goal of much LLT mercantile activity in West-Central Europe will have been quite specific. Roman engagements with trans-Alpine Europe were greatly shaped by this reality, with predictable consequences for countless peripheral groups that became faced with a choice to evade, resist, or participate in an expanding and lucrative trade in human captives.[1]

Just like the use of refuges and social pervasiveness of martial values among LHa and ELT groups is understood best in relation to growing slaver activity in Northwest Europe, the later LIA occupation of large defended settlements, adoption of high-value coinage, and prevalence of mounted warrior bands (Fernández-Götz 2014c: 215; Roymans 2007: 487) can likewise be understood in relation to the existence of a formal slave trade, with wine and wine-drinking paraphernalia playing a central function. Ethnographic comparison allows for a more nuanced understanding of such phenomena. Where this concerns the formation of martial sub-cultures, for example, research among afflicted West African communities demonstrates how such groups did not merely form reactively out of considerations of defense, but in order for boys and young men to survive disintegrating social systems (Klein 2001: 60). Similar institutions likely formed when comparable conditions arose in European contexts, such as early Medieval Ireland where male warrior bands (*fianna*) operated outside mainstream 'tribal' structures

---

[1] That indigenous groups participated in the slave trade cannot be denied (Avram 2007; Creighton 2000: 20; Lenski 2008: 91; Wilson 2012), and slavers will have been keen to collaborate with any locals willing and able to assist in the capture and transport of northern captives to Mediterranean markets.

(Creighton 2000: 20). A similar institution (*comitatus*) arose in the Celto-Germanic world, where patron-client arrangements were maintained between warrior leaders and their followers, relations that many likely did not voluntarily partake in (Lenski 2008: 88). Relevant, in this regard, is Tacitus' (*Germany* 31) description of a curious tradition among the trans-Rhenian Chatti, where young men were required to wear iron neck rings. This apparently signaled the wearer's subordinate (i.e. slave) status, a situation that could be improved by the killing of a foe. While the radical relativist would be content to report on this as an interesting cultural particularity, as Tacitus does, when we consider the detrimental effects of slaving on a society it is possible to recognize how such a 'tradition' might arise among groups where manipulating leaders exploit the minds and bodies of marginalized youths. From this point of view, the warrior band phenomenon succinctly captures the concurrent processes of social stratification and marginalization.

Indeed, it is not difficult to see how increasing numbers of people became socially and economically marginalized during the last decades of the pre-Roman Iron Age. Not simply in general terms because differentiation breeds inequality, but more directly in terms of the personal suffering and social disorder caused by slaving (Haselgrove 1987: 110). Here alcohol consumption can be considered for the way it will have contributed to deteriorating social conditions. The drinking of alcoholic beverages has of course been common throughout human history, and social scientists have long noted the psychological and social significance of alcohol consumption. However, it is also certainly true, as argued by Erchak, that this can reach ...

> 'problematic levels when people lose their sense of self-efficacy, when they feel hopeless and powerless against their environment and the future ... Is it just a coincidence, for example, that simple small-scale societies, many of whom have used indigenous alcoholic beverages for centuries, only begin to experience significant levels of problem drinking after loss of political sovereignty and economic self-sufficiency?' (Erchak 1992: 152).

The social consequences of an enduring exchange of slaves for alcohol has been demonstrated in various historical contexts (Arnold 1999; Curto 2004; Dietler 2006; Gustafsson 2005), and, in Iron Age Europe as well, an increased availability of storable alcohol likely contributed to deteriorating social conditions (Loughton 2009: 102),[2] with anomie and fatalism increasingly shaping worldviews, discourses, and behaviors (Mata 2017b: 129). The fact that a northern distributional limit of amphorae (Figure 8) corresponds with a reported resistance to wine and other imports among some North Gallic and trans-Rhenian groups (Caesar *Gallic Wars* II.15, IV.2) is perhaps a telling sign of the disruptive effects of slaving and alcohol consumption in the Celto-Germanic world of the LIA.[3] Diodorus' charge, that the Gaul's fondness for alcohol had them trade a slave for a jug of wine (*Library of History* V.26), while no doubt harboring strong cultural bias, may simultaneously point to rather depressing socio-economic realities.

Diodorus' comments belong to a kind of barbarian discourse that pervades ancient written sources. Historically, slave-owning groups have always maintained certain beliefs about the essential qualities of particular 'races' or ethnic groups, with enduring harassment a deplorable consequence (Gavriljuk 2003; Joshel 2010). That this drove exploited peoples into lasting destitution only legitimized enslavement in the eyes of their persecutors and future masters. References to barbarians selling their own into slavery

---

[2] Suggestively, the abandonment of farmsteads and occupation of large defended settlements in the Aisne valley (N France) between *c*. 150-120 BC coincided with the initial appearance of Republican wine amphorae (Loughton 2009: 87).

[3] Figure 8 shows a clear boundary beyond which wine was rarely exported north. The few finds in the northern part of the study area date to the Augustan era and likely arrived there with the earliest Roman legions. While wine may certainly have been transported north in wineskins instead of amphorae (Taylor 2001: 28), in the absence of any clear geographic obstacles that may have necessitated this, it is difficult to understand what may have limited distribution of amphorae further north other than a cultural resistance, as reported by ancient commentators.

(Diodorus *Library of History* V.26; Herodotus *Histories* 5.6; Philostratus *Life of Apollonius* VIII.7.12) reflect two important aspects in this regard: that the othering of the barbarian served to legitimize enslavement, and that commercial imperialism both encouraged and exploited those very forces of marginalization for which the victims of the slave trade themselves were blamed. Enslavers of marginalized people have always sought to legitimize their point-of-view by various sorts of rationalizations, from laymen stereotyping all the way to complex intellectual discourse (Heath 2008; Lavan 2013: 137; Lenski 2008: 84). Irrespective of its sophistication, the result is the radical othering of populations that were enduringly targeted for exploitation.

The comparative literature also shows how such attitudes encouraged extreme dehumanizing treatment of captives who commonly experienced punitive violence when attempting to resist what their exploiters invariably perceived as a legitimate ('natural') order of things (Graham 1965). In West-Central Europe, archaeological evidence for the discriminatory treatment of 'human cattle' (Bradley 1992: 129; Bradley 2000; Lavan 2013: 83) no doubt has long been hidden in plain sight. Mortuary deviance especially is a strong indicator for this (Ailincăi 2016; Murphy 2008; Perego 2014; Taylor 2008). Undoubtedly, the bodies of maltreated and murdered captives were disposed in ways that diverged from normative mortuary practices (e.g. lacking ceremony or grave goods, signs of malnutrition or mutilation, placed in isolation or odd positions). Evidence for atypical mortuary treatment of marginalized individuals is encountered in numerous historical contexts, and commonly in association with a slave trade (Martin and Akins 2001; Taylor 2005: 230).[4]

This is not to say that captives were always treated in ad hoc ways because violence certainly was also performed in highly ritualized ways (Baum 1999; Graham 1965; Ojo 2005). At sanctuary sites like Verbe Incarné (Lyon, France), ritual sacrifice is suggested by the co-presence of 'decapitated' wine amphorae and the severed skull of a woman (Fentress 2011: 65). Individuals like this may have been abused and killed ceremoniously not unlike those in the context of the Viking-Arab slave trade (Taylor 2005: 230). The occurrence of damaged and disarticulated human bones in numerous 'sacred' places of the Celto-Germanic world strongly point to non-sporadic ritualized violence (Aldhouse-Green 2004, 2005). In Southwest Germany, large numbers of human bones have also been found at hillforts of LHa and ELT date (Fernández-Götz and Krausse 2013: 478; Fiedler *et al.* 2009; Gronenborn 2001: 23), and at LIA *oppida* such finds are commonly recovered from ditches and pits, or found among surface refuse.[5] If not attributed to tribal warfare, such finds tend to be interpreted as evidence for ancestor worship (Fernández-Götz 2014a: 118; Fernández-Götz and Roymans 2015: 20), yet when human remains were left exposed in open pits and ditches, or put on display, this might instead point to public sacrificial rites that stressed alterity. Ritual sites like Gournay-sur-Aronde, Acy-Romance, and Ribemont-sur-Ancre (all in the Aisne-Marne region) have become altogether famous for the evidence they have provided for performative violence of this kind (Aldhouse-Green 2004: 333; Aldhouse-Green 2005: 156; Gronenborn 2001: 23; Wells 2002: 378).

Nonetheless, even at these infamous cult sites, ritual activity may actually have been shaped by quite profane motivations. To understand this better, it is important to distinguish between cults

---

[4] Also see note 74.
[5] Human remains of this sort are numerous at the Manching *oppidum* (Sievers 1999). These have also been found scattered among surface refuse at Altenburg-Rheinau, Breisach-Hochstetten, Marthalen, and Basel-Gasfabrik (Collis 1977: 8). Casual references to atypical depositions of human remains are numerous in the literature. Wells (1999: 81), for example, mentions the remains of a human skull found near the inner wall of the Kellheim *oppidum*, while human limb bones have also been recovered near the inner wall of the Engelhalbinsen *oppidum* (Wiedmer 1963). Vandenmoortele (2011: 147) mentions Bad-Neuheim where human remains are encountered across the entire surface area of the settlement. Fernández-Götz, in turn, notes that skull fragments were found near a ritual altar and within a surrounding ditch at the open assembly area of the contemporary Titelberg *oppidum* (Fernández-Götz 2014a: 113).

Republican (LT C-D) Amphoras

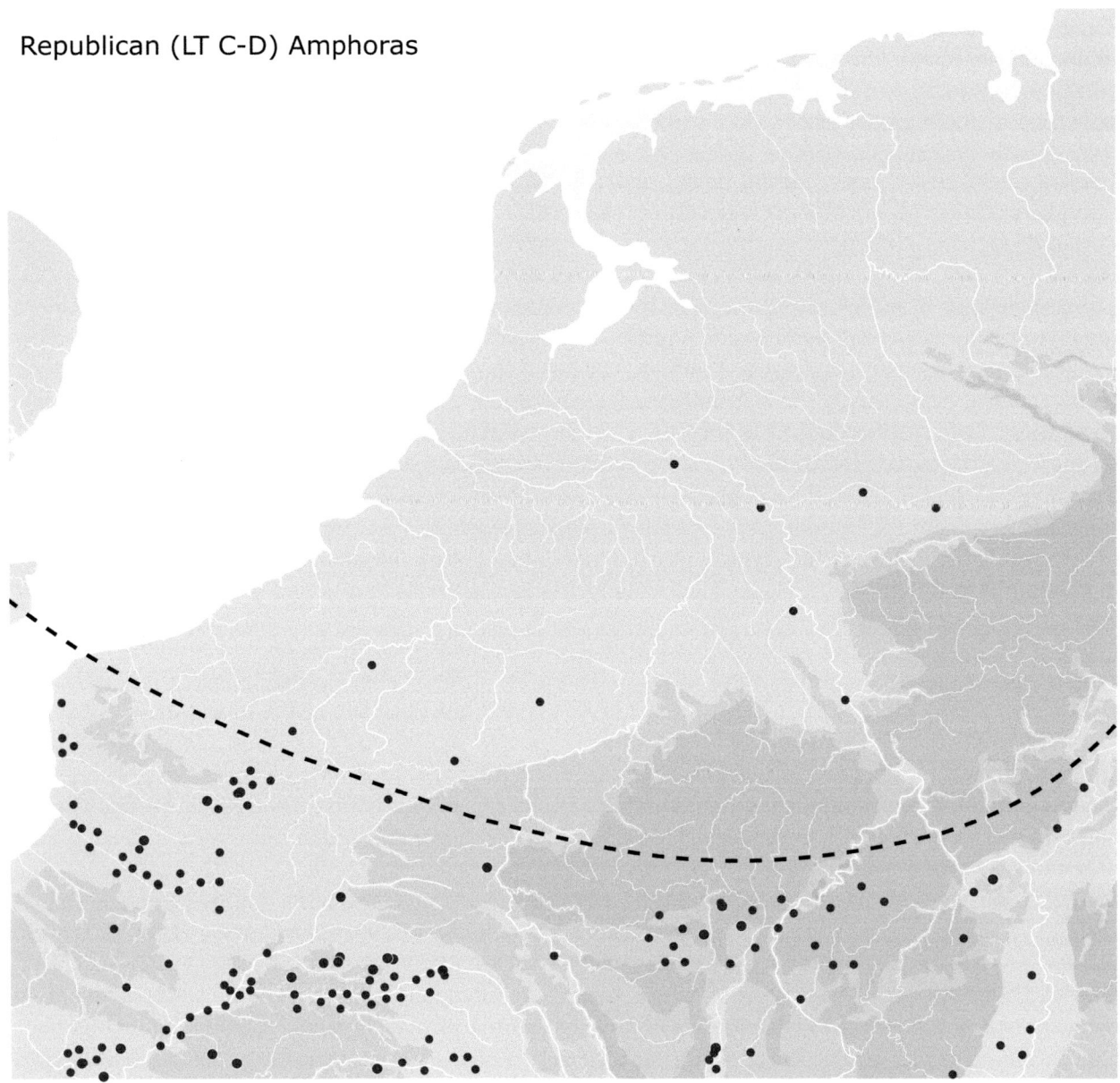

Figure 8: Distribution of Republican (LT C-D) amphorae (adapted from Loughton 2009 and Morris 2010)

that emphasize the importance of cyclical regeneration, and those where a symbolic focus rests disproportionately on violence and death. For the former we can expect a distributed focus on life and fertility, death and rebirth. But, if the only detectable cultic focus is violence and death – explicitly enacted through brutal acts of torture, dismemberment, and exposure – then other motivations are worth considering. For one, if ritualized violence at these prominent Aisne-Marne sites was motivated by security concerns, such that it involved sacrificing life in order to ensure its continuation, why did such practices not continue during a period of increased Roman imposition? That it was predominantly adult men who were sacrificed can perhaps be understood better when we consider the commercial interests of slavers. For those who captured and transported slaves, adult males were more troublesome and generally less profitable than women and children, resulting in disproportionate levels of violence directed towards adult men (DeBoer 2008: 239). Moreover, terrorizing captives by exposing them to the abuse and murder of their kin was a brutally effective way of forcing submission and easing transport to distant markets (Cameron and Martin 2012: 5).[6]

That violence was often committed in highly ritualized ways is beyond doubt, but this does not mean that it could not simultaneously be motivated by highly pragmatic concerns. As those who have critiqued the modern habit of primitivizing past practices have argued (Arnold 2011: 162), archaeological interpretation of difficult to understand human behavior too commonly moves into the realm of the sacred, whereby ritual significance is too readily ascribed. Thus, children with malformed bodies are believed to have been killed ceremonially because such individuals threatened a socio-cosmic order (Aldhouse-Green 2004, 2005). Yet, it is not altogether certain whether physically distorted individuals were actually perceived in such ways. Indeed, evidence for medical knowledge and healing practices in later prehistory (Moghaddam *et al.* 2015) suggest that a tolerance for physical deformity may have been greater than supposed.[7] Nor is it certain that female sexual promiscuity, another scenario that has been put forward, would have been seen as transgressive in broadly egalitarian societies because these are precisely the kinds of cultural contexts where we can expect greater gender equality. Moreover, for some individuals 'sacrificed' in the swampy places of northern Europe (i.e. 'bog-bodies'), evidence suggests that the perpetrators of these violent acts were rather ill-prepared for ritual ceremony; that some captives were bound and throttled with their own clothes and belts points instead to a degree of improvisation. This seems to go unrecognized precisely because of this preference for interpreting brutal acts of violence as ritualistic and guided by socio-cosmic beliefs. Alternative explanations that foreground motivations like male gang cohesion or economic profit remain unconsidered (Taylor 2005: 230). Foregrounding the slave trade, then, urges new questions to be asked. Did inaccessible marshlands offer refuge to those unable to resist raiding parties?[8] Had a woman been left staked to the ground as a brutal punitive measure because she resisted being forcibly taken from her homeland? Were the elderly and the deformed ruthlessly disposed after a raid because no profit could be gained from them? Was the blond hair of some captives removed because this was a profitable commodity on Mediterranean markets (Bartman 2001)?

Evidence of this kind shows how distinct attitudes and behaviors formed in pronounced ways among slavers, with violence a characteristic aspect. Yet, these existed outside ceremonial settings as well, shaping various aspects of life and becoming expressed in different social contexts. It has long been observed that strong ideas about personal and collective autonomy commonly developed within slave-owning societies. I already noted how the Greek demand for slaves increased significantly at a time when strong democratizing processes were manifesting there. As socio-historical realities changed across West-Central Europe during the Iron Age, new norms and ideals shaped by binary constructs like self-other, servant-master, distinction-equality, and harmony-conflict will have gained significance (Lavan 2013: 75; Scheidel 2008: 117). The valorization of personal autonomy may have become more pronounced precisely because of a strong conceptual distinction between freedom and enslavement. As Taylor notes, the well-attested interest for torc symbolism throughout Iron Age Europe can perhaps best be understood as 'a reflex of the existence of slave chains' (2001: 39). It indeed seems possible that

---

[6] Similarly, causing terror was an important tactic of slave raiders seeking to harvest catchment areas in the long-term. Not only was it necessary to overcome local resistance during any particular incursion, punishment needed to be severe enough as to terrorize target groups into believing that any future attempt at organized resistance was highly unwise. The mutilation and murder of adult males could achieve this.
[7] Notably, the famous Vix 'princess', interred in one of the most opulent (HA D-LT A) burials in the West Hallstatt world, seems to have been physically deformed (Arnold 2011: 163), but this apparently did not adversely affect her status.
[8] Caesar reports how groups inhabiting the Dutch and Belgian coastal regions tended to seek refuge in forests and swamps (*Gallic Wars* III.28). Ancient observers not uncommonly comment on the barbarian's ability to survive inhospitable environments (Cassius Dio *Roman History* 77.12.1-4), yet, it is likely that incessant slave raiding commonly forced people to abandon productive environments and inhabit more marginal and isolated areas like marshlands and mountainous landscapes.

within some communities torcs signaled subservience to a deity, ethnic group, or lineage, sacred bonds that no real-world enslavement could undo (Aldhouse-Green 2004: 328; Arnold 2011: 157; Taylor 2005: 231).

That metal neck rings (along with amber and glass adornments) were predominantly worn by women during LT A in the Aisne-Marne region might indicate that such constructs also could become highly gendered. While gender ideals have of course varied significantly across time and space, cross-cultural regularities can certainly be recognized. Where this concerns the cultural valuation of women, for example, distinct norms and ideals have long manifested within strongly stratified societies (de Beauvoir 1968), especially those with institutionalized systems of servitude like ancient Greece and Rome (Bauman 1992; Blundell 1995; Pomeroy 1975). Within such societies, women are commonly venerated as keepers of house and hearth, and as custodians of family lineages. Similarly, gendered constructs are also attested among slavers, where women are highly valued as tokens of wealth or prestige. Illustrative are the observations of the 10th century AD Arabic traveler Ibn Fadlān who wrote …

> 'I saw the Rus, who had come for trade and camped by the river Itil … Round their necks, [their women] wear torques of gold and silver, for every man, as soon as he accumulates 10,000 dirhams, has a torque made for his wife. When he has 20,000, he has two torques made [and so on] … With them, there are beautiful slave girls, for sale to the merchants' (Fadlān 2012: 45).

In the study area, the contemporaneous initial arrival of chariots and Mediterranean glass during LT A perhaps suggests the manifestation of just such constructs there. If slaves were expressly exchanged for glass, it is quite possible that objects made of this material became imbued with strong ideological significance, not unlike torcs. Glass bracelets are ubiquitous in LT C-D settlement assemblages, especially in the northern part of the study area where they predominantly occur in the graves of women (Roymans and Verniers 2010) (Figure 11). Despite their fragile nature, and the distant provenance of the raw material, these objects seem to have been worn quite regularly by women, such that we can expect certain ideals concerning female behavior and comportment to have spread as well. Perhaps women who wore fragile body ornaments so frequently were not expected to lead very active lives? If so, manual labor may mainly have been performed by those who did not (or were not allowed to) adorn themselves with glass bracelets.[9]

Among those groups enduringly targeted by slavers, certain ideals and beliefs will have manifested that allowed for the psychological negotiation of a perilous existence. The abduction of women and children not only resulted in immeasurable personal suffering, it also will have had tragic consequences at a societal level. Consider, for example, how the removal of women and girls signified the end of entire family lineages in a matrilineal society (Arnold 1999: 83; Fernández-Götz 2014c: 101; Pope and Ralston 2011: 382). It is not difficult to imagine, then, how family-centric ideals concerning descent, protection, and perpetuity became increasingly prioritized, something archaeological research in the study area has adequately shown (Mata 2017b: 211). Changes in both mortuary and settlement contexts strongly suggest that an ideological outlook that idealized the autonomous family and its lineage first arose in the Rhine-Moselle and Aisne-Marne regions, and then some time later in the Scheldt-Meuse region. This ideological centrality of the family then continued to be expressed for centuries in the Roman northwest provinces through mortuary and cultic expressions.

---

[9] In the Dutch central river area, grave sites of EIA and MIA date show a clear distinction between cremation burials that contain no grave goods, and inhumation burials in which women with various bodily adornments were interred (Vleeshouwer 2012). It is difficult to determine, however, whether the cremation rite reflects egalitarian or differentiating ideals. Does the absence of grave goods signify membership in an undifferentiated society or does it point to the existence of a subservient class? Was inhumation reserved for high-status women, or low-status but high-value slaves?

The central point to make here is that any examination of socio-cultural transformation in the study area has to consider the impact of slaving and enslavement, which, despite geographic and temporal variability in scale, intensity, and operation, endured for centuries and expanded significantly in the last decades of the pre-Roman Iron Age. To reiterate, those groups inhabiting this part of Europe throughout the long Iron Age had little to exchange for Mediterranean luxuries apart from human captives (Dietler 1989: 133; Gronenborn 2001: 4; Nash-Briggs 2002: 166; Nash-Briggs 2003: 248; Roymans 2004: 22; Roymans 2007: 489). It is highly likely that Aisne-Marne warlords of the EIA, in particular, became heavily involved in a trade in human captives (Nash 1985: 53; Nash-Briggs 2003: 255),[10] and, centuries later, those groups that engaged in ritualized violence at the infamous sanctuaries of Gournay-sur-Aronde, Acy-Romance, and Ribemont-sur-Ancre likely controlled a cross-channel slave trade that brought British captives to the continent.[11] It is among Aisne-Marne and Rhine-Moselle groups – two core areas of La Tène cultural effervescence – where archaeologists have found clear evidence for significant social change. Hilltop refuges were predominantly built in these two areas, initially perhaps by groups keen on defending themselves from foreign slavers, but eventually by those who came to participate in the trade. It is also amongst these communities that we find the strongest signs for political centralization and social differentiation during the two centuries before the Roman conquest, and where a number of large permanently occupied defended settlements (*oppida*) were built. Also in the southern parts of the study area, rural settlements (Figures 9 and 10) show the tell-tale signs of private land ownership and interest for strict spatial planning (enclosing and movement control) (Haselgrove 2007), while the regional production and distribution of coins and craft objects (brooches and pottery), together with the widespread occurrence of Mediterranean imports (wine amphorae and bronze wares), suggest that coin-based commerce was spreading rapidly during the LIA.

These developments in the southern half of the study area stand in stark contrast to the situation in the North. There, archaeologists find little evidence for social stratification or the rise of larger political formations until the arrival of Caesar's legions (51-58 BC). Northern communities were highly geared towards self-sufficiency and weakly integrated. There is no evidence for communal refuges or defended settlements. Instead, open farmsteads and small farming settlements remained the dominant forms of habitation throughout the entire Iron Age (Gerritsen 2003; Roymans 1996). While it is true that goods from other regions consistently reached these parts (Roymans 2009), this never occurred in substantial quantities. There are also no strong signs for economic specialization, surplus production, centralized storage, or market exchange. Non-commercial high-value coins were only minted locally in the last decades before the Roman conquest (Roymans and Aarts 2009). It is also at this late pre-Roman stage that a very limited interest developed for settlement nucleation, enclosing, and partitioning (Arnoldussen and Jansen 2010: 388). These are the first indications for social differentiation in the North, a development that intensified rapidly when all territories south of the Rhine became incorporated into the Roman state.

---

[10] Nash-Briggs suggests that Aisne-Marne warlords may have brought northern slaves to places like Mont Lassois (Burgundy, France) where Mediterranean goods arrived during the later sixth century BC. Centers like Mont Lassois may have served as transshipment points where northern slaves were transported along the Seine or Aube Rivers in a southeasterly direction towards the Saône-Rhône River.

[11] Literary references that identify Britain as a source for slaves support this notion (Cicero *Letters to Atticus* 4.17.303; Strabo *Geography* IV 5.2). Archaeologists have also wondered whether large parts of Iron Age Britain, particularly those areas where hillforts were numerous, may have served as raiding grounds for slave traders (Creighton 2000: 20; Cunliffe 1997: 220). It is tempting, then, to compare evidence for human sacrifice discovered along the Thames River (Bradley and Gordon 1988) with that from sacrificial sites in the study area (e.g. Gournay-sur-Aronde, Acy-Romance, and Ribemont-sur-Ancre). Furthermore, literary reports on the cultural practice of polyandry in pre-Roman Britain (Caesar *Gallic Wars* 5.14; Cassius Dio *Roman History* 77.12.1-4) are interesting because such a presumed cultural tradition may have arisen due to the demographic consequences of recurring slaving activity. For comparison, Dalton and Leung (2011) argue that the prevalence of polygyny among Early Modern West African groups may have been a consequence of the Atlantic slave trade that caused a shortage of men.

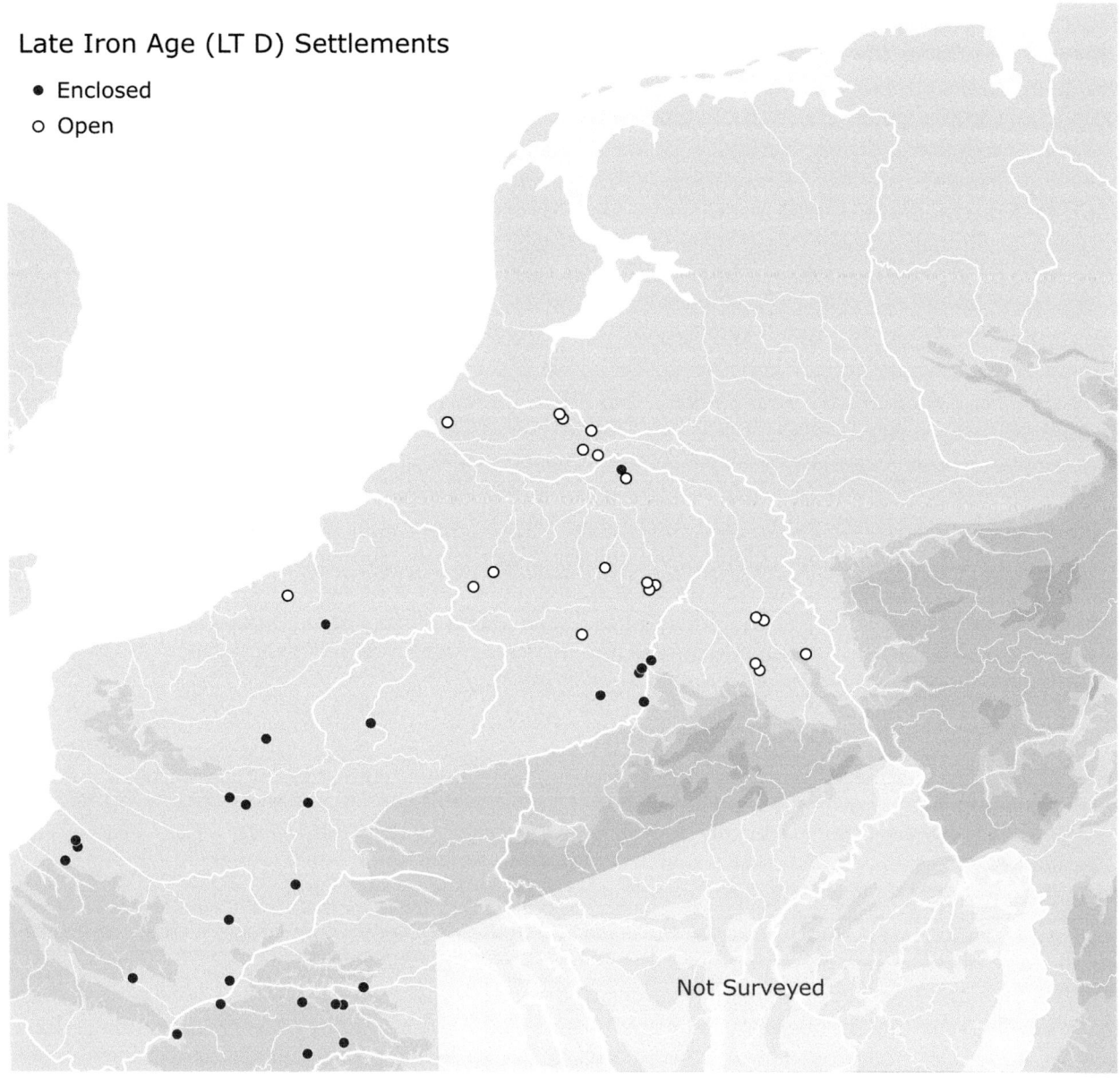

Figure 9: Distribution of LT D enclosed and open settlements (adapted from Roymans and Habermehl 2011)

This clear divergence between northern and southern developments allows proposing that groups inhabiting the northern lowland regions – where environmental marginality, low economic productivity, and egalitarian ideals may have hindered inter-group cooperation (e.g. construction of refuges, military alliances) – were particularly vulnerable to the excesses of a slave trade. Throughout the long Iron Age, northern regions may variably (in terms of intensity and scale) but enduringly have served as a catchment area for slavers belonging to Rhine-Moselle and Aisne-Marne groups. This situation may only have changed over the course of the first century BC when some communities finally managed to thwart exploitation, likely by becoming participants in the trade.[12] Lower Rhineland groups like the

---

[12] Braund and Tsetskhladze (1989) note how banditry and piracy could become an important survival strategy for groups challenged by environmental constraints and depressed socio-economic conditions. In similar terms, Gavriljuk (2003: 77) argues how the barbarian steppe societies north of the Black Sea region could only offer slaves in return for Mediterranean luxuries, and a similar argument is made by Wrenhaven (2013: 9) for the region to the east of the Black Sea (Colchis).

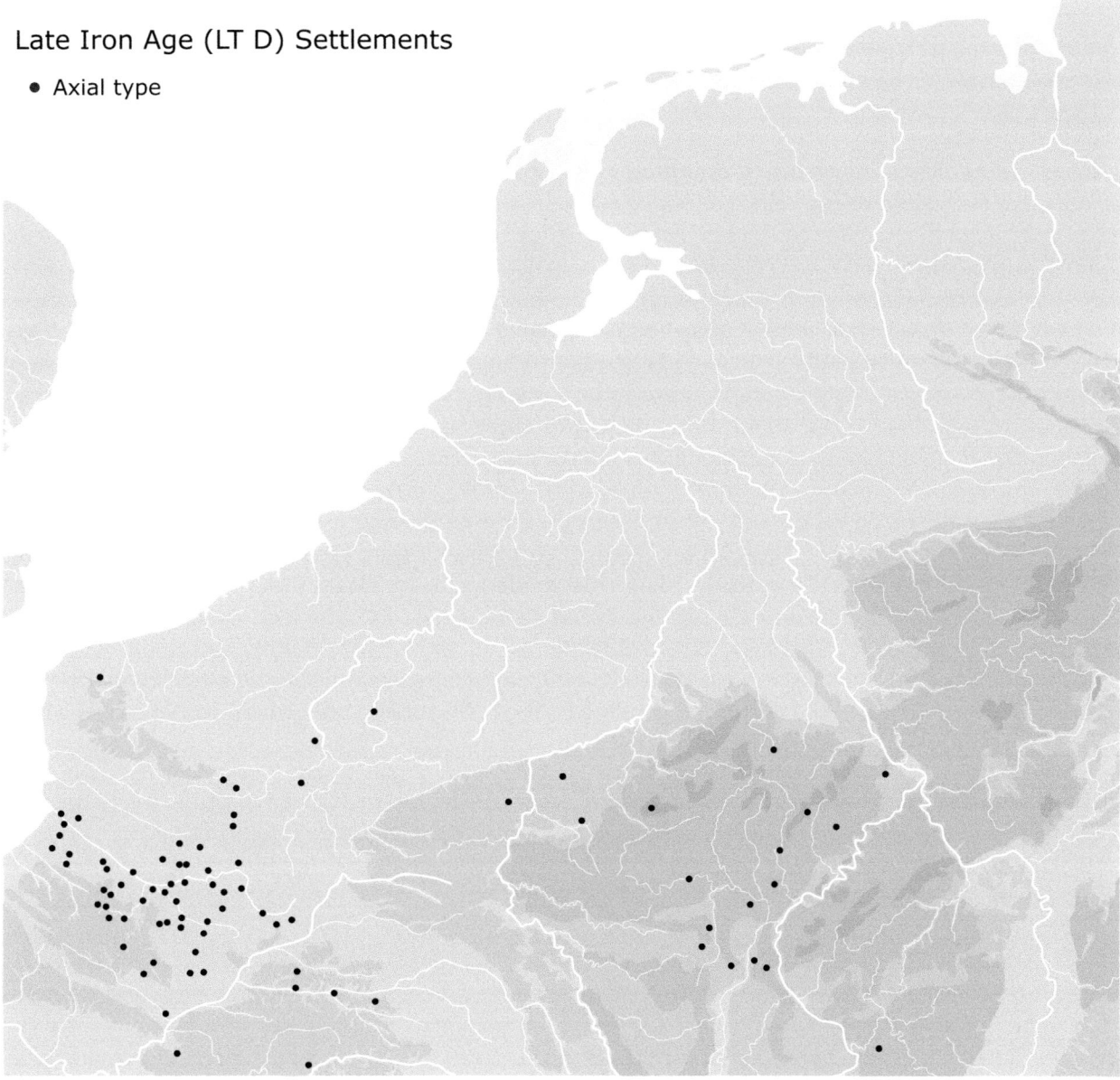

Figure 10: Distribution of LT D axial settlements (adapted from Roymans and Habermehl 2011)

Eburones, and the Batavi after them (Figure 12), may have started supplying trans-Rhenian captives to southern groups that are known to have maintained friendly relations with Rome, like the Remi in the Aisne-Marne region and the Treveri in the Rhine-Moselle region (Roymans 2009: 221).[13] Different kinds of archaeological evidence (coinage, weapons, horse gear, and communal cult sites) associated with these Lower Rhineland groups do indeed point to the adoption of new materials and practices, and the rise of new kinds of social arrangements. However, because this mainly relates to a distinct phenomenon – namely, young men participating in the raiding expeditions of 'warrior elites' – these are hardly signs of substantial social transformation. Likewise, for segmentary groups inhabiting coastal

---

[13] Such a scenario fits Caesar's (*Gallic Wars* IV.6, V.27) claims that the Eburones were clients of the Treveri. Research at the Titelberg *oppidum* has shown how this important Treveran settlement 'experienced its greatest period of economic and commercial activity in the decades following [Caesar's conquests], with vast numbers of luxury imports brought in from Italy and from Southern Gaul' (Wells 2002: 381).

regions, there is no evidence for significant social change, such that we can expect these communities to have remained vulnerable to exploitation. This was a situation that only worsened in subsequent centuries for those indigenous communities situated in Rome's cross-frontier harassment zone (Mata 2017a: 8).[14]

Further archaeological evidence substantiates this proposition of trans-Rhenian territories having served as a slave catchment area. Beginning with numismatic data, it seems suggestive that high-value gold coins first arrived in the northern half of the study area from a SW (Aisne-Marne) and a SE (Rhine-Moselle) direction during the second century BC (Roymans and Aarts 2009). When we consider the historical circumstances of their initial use in the Celto-Germanic world – namely, payment of mercenaries by Hellenistic rulers (Haselgrove 1984, 1999) – it is not difficult to see how high-value coins could have been minted and distributed specifically to fund slave raiding campaigns. To imagine how this may have worked a useful comparison can be drawn to the Viking assembly known as the '*Thing*' (Fernández-Götz 2014a: 120). Significantly, it was at these annual springtime meetings that Viking communities planned raiding expeditions. It stands to reason that similar events were organized by Iron Age groups, and likewise commemorated by special-issue coins.[15] Especially when coin symbolism made clear reference to shared beliefs and values this could serve as an effective means of securing loyalties. Indeed, coins used for commemoration and recruitment were ideal portable media for communicating shared interests and ideals through well-known symbolic imagery (Mata 2017a: 21). That the use of high-value-coins can be linked to slaving is perhaps also suggested by the fact that the earliest (mid-second century BC) coin imports in the Scheldt-Meuse region are immediately associated with gold torcs (Fernández-Götz 2014c: 214; Roymans 2007: 479). Coin emissions were not minted in the northern half of the study area until the mid-first century BC (60-30 BC), when local groups likely became active participants in the international slave trade.[16]

Apart from numismatic information we can again consider the distribution of glass bracelets because it points to the existence of a boundary zone in the Lower Rhineland region (Figure 11). If the notion of a trans-Rhenian slave catchment area can be accepted, then the fact that the highest concentration of the earliest La Tène bracelets in trans-Alpine Europe can be found exactly on its southern boundary is suggestive of a possible role in this distinct trade (Gerritsen and Roymans 2006: 263). The earliest arrival of glass bracelets there has been dated to the second half of the third century BC (LT C). Because this is quite close to their initial mid-third century BC appearance in Central Europe (Roymans and Verniers 2010: 204), this may have resulted from rather targeted exchange efforts.[17] Since the raw glass used in the manufacture of these objects was imported from Eastern Mediterranean sources (Roymans *et al.* 2014), it becomes possible to envision a trade whereby Mediterranean merchants or Central European middle-men sought to exchange glass for trans-Rhenian slaves in the Lower Rhineland. From there they were transported south (Saône-Rhône route) and east (Danube route) to Mediterranean markets. Furthermore, this was a trade that Rhine-Moselle groups in particular could have sought to control

---

[14] There may also have been groups that actively resisted slave trading, like the Nervii, of whom Caesar (*Gallic Wars* II-15) reported that they did not allow southern merchants with their corrupting goods to enter their territory.

[15] Supporting this idea of the Treveri having been active in the slave trade is the fact that Treveran coins were minted at at least four *oppida*, namely Donnersberg, Martberg, Titelberg, and Wallendorf (Fernández-Götz 2014c: 155).

[16] It is in relation to these developments that we can perhaps also understand the expansion of horsemanship in the Lower Rhineland during the LIA (Gerritsen and Roymans 2006: 256). Those Lower Rhineland groups that consequently came to serve in the Roman military were lauded for their ability to pursue their quarry on horseback through aquatic environments (Hassell 1970), skills they undoubtedly developed at an earlier time.

[17] Finds from EIA and MIA burials in the Dutch central river area, in particular the dress items found in the graves of women, point to linkages with Central Europe (Vleeshouwer 2012: 13), as does the evidence for horse gear from EIA chieftain's graves found in Belgium and the Netherlands (Egg 2017: 60).

Glass '7-ribbed' Bracelets

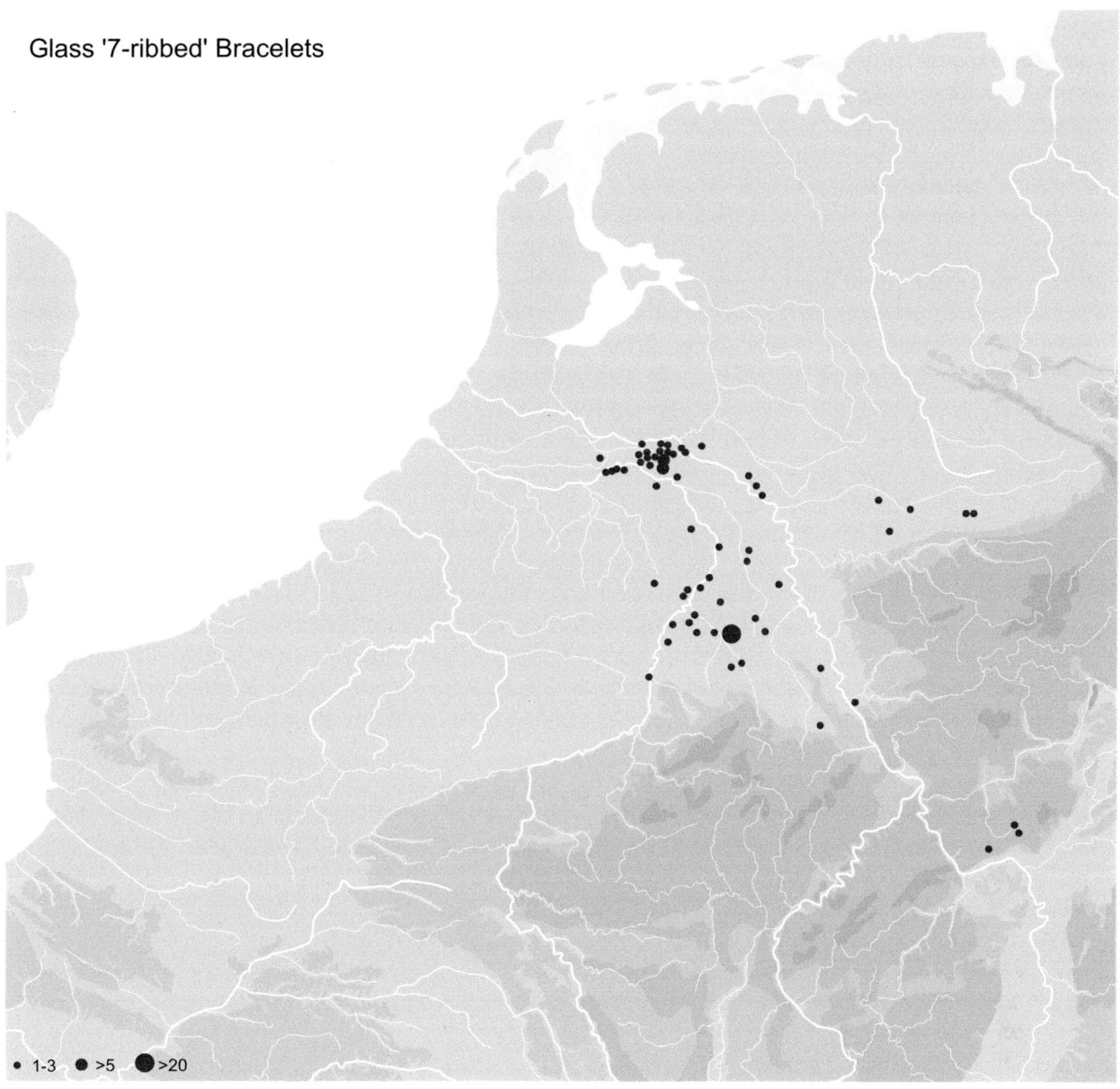

Figure 11: Distribution of LT C glass bracelets (adapted from Roymans and Verniers 2010: 204)

during LT D.[18] The comparative-ethnographic literature also shows how such a restricted trade could develop, and, intriguingly, glass (beads) also became a material favored by Early Modern European merchants for acquiring slaves in Africa where it was highly valued by certain indigenous groups (Gronenborn 2001; Guerrero 2010).

---

[18] Again, that the Eburones were considered clients of the Treveri aligns with this idea. Circulation of La Tène glass bracelets halted rather abruptly in the Augustan period (44 BC-AD 14), when these items disappear from the archaeological record. When Roman expansionism upset existing socio-economic systems, this undoubtedly included the trade in human captives. Whether because slavers attached themselves to Roman legions or because Roman leadership actively sought to repress their involvement, the participation of indigenous groups in the slave trade was disrupted. This, then, might explain the abrupt halt to the circulation of glass bracelets in the study area.

It is possible to elaborate further on this notion of a northern slave catchment area having been exploited by southern groups if we consider the incidental evidence for hair removal from bog bodies, which, I hinted above, may in certain cases be understood better with the interests of slavers in mind. Human attitudes towards hair and hair styles are strongly linked to ideology and identity, something that is amply demonstrated by Roman written sources, which also happen to comment on the beliefs and practices of Celto-Germanic groups. Hair was a powerful signaling device for communicating cultural identity; for example, Roman men characteristically kept their hair short, especially in military context, while 'true' Germans could ostensibly be recognized by their long locks. The practice of wearing long hair in a particular style of knot could reportedly be used to distinguish Suebian men from other Germans (Tacitus *Germany* 38); that particular practice likely also signaled social status because slaves were prohibited from doing so. For some Germanic groups it is also reported that the heads of women were shaved in punishment for adultery (Tacitus *Germany* 19); in Roman society it was runaway and manumitted slaves who suffered a similar treatment (Aldhouse-Green 2004: 335). Also in Rome, the wearing of blond wigs seems to have been associated with subservience and subjugation; prostitutes were required by law to make use of them, while defeated enemies could signal their capitulation symbolically by surrendering their hair (*captivos crines*). Reality mixes with imperial discourse here, as it was from subjugated populations that human hair was sourced to supply Roman wig manufacturing (Bartman 2001).

Notably, all this does not seem to have stopped Roman women from bleaching their hair or donning blond or red wigs, as social critics were keen to point out. Ovid's writings are particularly revealing here. In an attempt to ridicule the narcissism of Roman women who over-indulged in self-styling, the poet wrote how 'some poor German girl, the bounty of our conquest in that barbaric land' provided the blond hair of which wigs were made, further asking 'will you confess the truth that the praise should go to some unknown Sygambrian woman?' (*Amores* 1.14). The poet wrote these words at a time when Roman legions were conquering Germanic lands, where the Sigambri were situated on the east bank of the Rhine (North Rhine-Westphalia, Germany). Ovid also mentions the concoctions used by Roman women to dye their hair, and, remarkably, the three products known to us – Batavian foam (*spuma Batava*), Chattian foam (*spuma Chaticca*), and Mattiacian soap (*pilae Mattiacae*) – all reference Germanic groups situated in the study area (Olson 2008: 73). The Batavi, Chatti, and Mattiaci were related groups that inhabited areas in the Lower and Middle Rhineland, with the Sigambri occupying territory just north of the Chatti (Figure 12).[19] Slavers will of course have been interested in manipulating the appearance of their captives in order to increase their market value,[20] and Roman writers certainly complained about the deplorable habit of slave traders for concealing flaws through beautification (Bodel 2005: 192;

---

[19] It is worth mentioning the Cananefates here. This Lower Rhineland group reportedly descended from the Batavi, and were therefore related to both the Chatti and the Mattiaci (Tacitus *Histories* IV.15.1; Tacitus *Germany* XXIX). During the first century BC and AD, the Cananefates occupied territory west of the Batavi (Figure 12). The meaning of their name is typically understood to have meant 'leek-masters'. While it might be thought to have been a externally imposed derogatory designation – in the vein of 'poor leek-eater' or 'dirty leek-grower' – I am inclined to a different interpretation if we can accept that the Cananefates might have been known for their slave-trading activities, like their Batavian, Mattiacian, and Chattian brethren. Markey (2013) has convincingly shown that 'leek' was commonly used in a number of languages to communicate ideas relating to sexual vigor and fertility. It was also commonly used as a euphemism for 'nubile woman'. From this point of view, being known as 'leek-masters' (i.e. owners and suppliers of beautiful young women) undoubtedly was meant as a compliment and not a slight.

[20] Here it is possible to offer a different perspective on the well-attested Bronze and Iron Age practice of depositing toiletry implements in 'warrior graves'. Such objects are quite commonly found interred with male individuals and linked to body care practices and the construction of 'male identities' (Eckardt and Crummy 2008; Kincade 2014). If it can be accepted that some of these 'chiefs' or 'warrior elites' had been active slave traders, it becomes possible to understand how such tools may have been used for slave beautification.

Harrill 2006: 130). It is tempting to imagine here how groups known for sourcing northern regions for fair-haired maidens also became infamous for concocting products for beautification.[21]

Communal 'cult places', or 'sanctuaries', constitute a context of social practice that may also be considered for its relevance to the slave trade. While this type of site is predominantly found in the southern half of the study area (Roymans 1990: 64), several have in recent years been recognized in the Dutch central river area.[22] It is commonly argued that these LT D cult places functioned as regional sites where communal ceremonies were staged by aspirational elites, while also serving the reproduction of (sub-)ethnic communities. Throughout the study area, many such sites continued functioning into the Roman period when they became prominent foci of Gallo-Roman religious activity. For LIA groups, cultic activity seemed to have centered on feasting and the ritual deposition of objects like weapons, coins, and metal dress items. I already suggested an alternative interpretation for some ritual sites, in particular those that provide evidence for human sacrifice. Of the numerous cult sites discovered in the study area, a significant portion has provided evidence for damaged human remains. These are commonly found in ditches or scattered among surface finds.[23] Most cult places with human remains are situated in the southwestern part of the study area, but it is quite possible that these are also present at sites where unidentified bone material has been found. In the North, one prominent cult place where people seemed to have engaged in ritual violence was discovered near present-day Kessel-Lith, at the confluence of the rivers Meuse and Waal (Gerritsen and Roymans 2006: 257; Roymans 2007: 482). Many metal finds (coins, weapons, dress items) were retrieved from the riverbed there, as well as the skeletal remains of adult males that show clear signs of violence.

Because of the possible participation of northern groups in a slave trade that brought trans-Rhenian captives to southern markets, it is worth reconsidering the characterization of these sites as 'cultic' or 'sacred'. To reiterate, there is no convincing evidence for social complexification in the northern part of the study area, not from settlement nor from mortuary contexts, until the very end of the LT D period. In other words, there was no normative socio-cultural framework in place that warrants an interpretation of sites like Kessel-Lith as cult places of regional importance where elites vied for social prominence by staging communal ceremonies. If we instead consider the practical aspects of a slave trade, it becomes possible to reinterpret these kinds of ritual sites as transshipment centers. To get a sense of how such a settlement might have functioned we can again consider observations made by Ibn Fadlān who described the activities of Viking slave traders at river-side ports-of-trade:

> 'As soon as their boats arrive at this port, each of them disembarks … and prostrates himself before a great idol, saying to it: 'Oh my lord, I have come from a far country and I have with me such and such a number of young slave girls, and such and such a number of sable skins … I would like you to do the favor of sending me a merchant who has large quantities of dinars and dirhams and who will buy everything that I want and not argue with me over my price' (Fadlān 2012: 45).

---

[21] Many of these pre-conquest practices and ideals seemed to have survived into the Early Roman period. Illustrative in this regard are some of the details relating to the Batavian revolt (AD 69-70) against the Romans. The Batavian leader Julius Civilis reportedly dyed his hair red and vowed to let it grow long in an act of defiance (Tacitus *History* IV.61). In his discussion of Batavian grievances that triggered the uprising, Tacitus lists the travesties committed by those in charge of executing a compulsory military levy. Among them, notably, the abuse of the elderly and the youthful for the respective purposes of collecting bribes and sexual exploitation. It is telling that the Batavian's fate is compared here to that of a slave (Tacitus *History* IV.14).

[22] These include sites at Elst, Empel-de Werf, Haren-Spaanse Steeg, Lith-Oijensche Hut, Maren-Kessel, Oss-Ussen, Roermond, and Rossum-Alem, all of which date between c. 130-50 BC (Jansen *et al.* 2002: 53).

[23] Roymans (1990: 63) lists six ritual sites where human remains have been found: Epiais-Rhus (skulls), Estrées-Saint-Denis (loose bones and complete skeletons, Digeon (various bones), Moeuvres (disarticulated skeletons of c. 200 individuals), Ribemont-sur-Ancre (various articulated and disarticulated bones of c. 200 individuals), and Gournay-sur-Aronde (disarticulated and damaged bones of c. 12 adults).

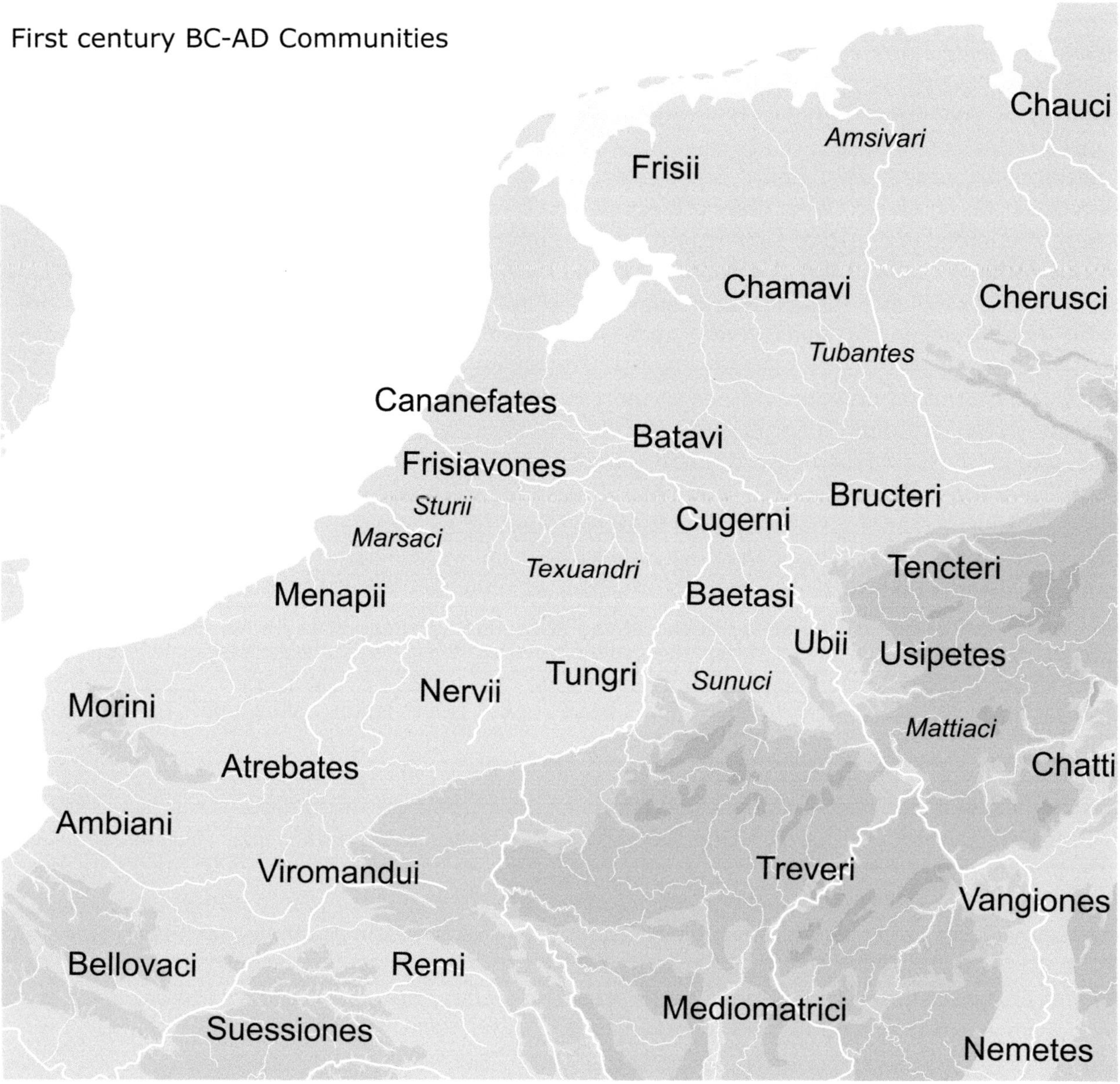

First century BC-AD Communities

![Map of first century BC-AD communities showing tribal names including Chauci, Frisii, Amsivari, Chamavi, Cherusci, Tubantes, Cananefates, Batavi, Frisiavones, Sturii, Marsaci, Texuandri, Cugerni, Bructeri, Menapii, Baetasi, Tencteri, Nervii, Tungri, Sunuci, Ubii, Usipetes, Morini, Mattiaci, Atrebates, Chatti, Ambiani, Viromandui, Treveri, Vangiones, Bellovaci, Remi, Suessiones, Mediomatrici, Nemetes]

Figure 12: Known communities in the study area during the first century BC and AD

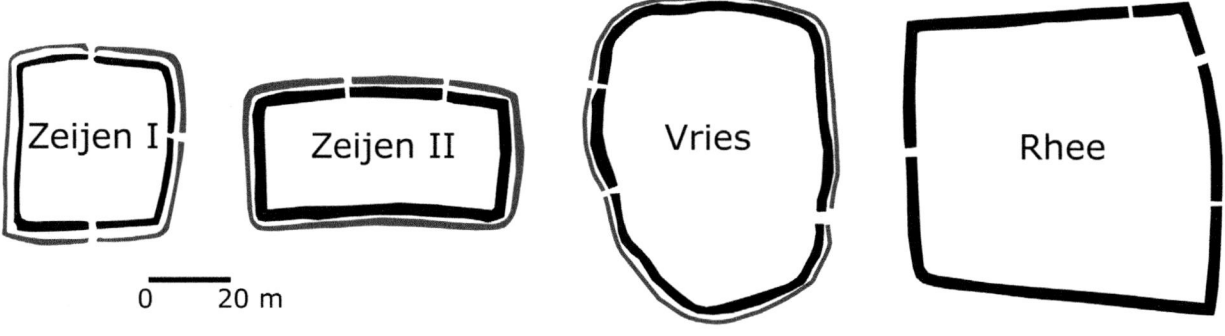

Figure 13: Schematic representations of LT C-D trans-Rhenian 'walled enclosures' (adapted from Waterbolk 1977)

Economic and religious interests were clearly entwined here, and this certainly was not unique to the Arab-Viking slave trade. In the Greco-Roman world, both spheres were also strongly entangled (Fernández-Götz 2014a: 112; Krämer 2016; Rauh 1993; Silver 1992). In the absence of international law and enforceable mercantile norms, tying commercial activity to religious ideas and rituals had obvious benefits. The various ideological, behavioral, and structural elements of long-distance commercial systems allowed for relations of trust to coagulate around shared beliefs, for people to adhere to behavioral norms, and for facilities situated at nodal points in transport networks to be used by merchants with diverse backgrounds (Grout 2016). Many LIA cult places in West-Central Europe might perhaps best be interpreted as spaces where commercial exchanges could take place under the watchful eyes of mutually recognized divine powers.

If this economic function of sacred places can be accepted, then the notion of captives being moved south through transshipment sites like Kessel-Lith becomes more palatable. Being situated in the Dutch central river area allowed its operators easy access to a trans-Rhenian catchment area.[24] This is perhaps further substantiated by the presence there of walled enclosures at present-day Zeijen, Vries, and Rhee that were contemporary (late second-early first century BC) with the transshipment site at Kessel-Lith (Arnoldussen and Jansen 2010: 389; Waterbolk 1977). Archaeologists have been reluctant to interpret these enclosures as fortified farmsteads because they are quite different from contemporary rural settlements that have been excavated in the area (Figure 13). They also do not seem to have been places of refuge because their proximity to prehistoric roadways suggests that connectivity was more important than isolation. It could be proposed, then, that they functioned as holding facilities where captives were temporarily detained for short periods of time before being transported to sites like Kessel-Lith.

That this proposition approaches past realities is further suggested by a contemporary population decline in the region where these walled enclosures were located. It certainly seems conceivable that intermittent but enduring slave raiding resulted in a demographic decline. Indeed, it may not have been coincidental that the emergence of artificial dwelling mounds (*terpen*) in the northern coastal regions of the Netherlands and Germany during the sixth century BC (Ha D) coincided with the arrival of material culture from Central Europe (Fokkens 1998: 127).[25] Since marginal coastal environments continued to be settled during the MIA (LT A-B), enduring insecurity from slaving may have continued to compel people to avoid settling inland areas that were more suitable for agricultural exploitation (Arnoldussen and Jansen 2010: 380; van Gijn and Waterbolk 1984). Similar processes may have occurred in the Aisne-Marne and Rhine-Moselle regions where a period (LT A) in which the largest number of chariots was interred over the course of two to three generations also ended in a demographic decline (Fernández-Götz 2016: 3), most noticeably in the intermediate Ardennes region.[26] Another population vacuum has been recognized in southern Germany where several large *oppida* were abandoned around the middle of the first century BC. In fact, countless of these large defended settlements in West-Central Europe seem to have been abandoned during the second half of the first century BC, but whether this can be linked to slaving has yet to be considered (Fernández-Götz 2014c: 230; Wells 2005: 60). While it is true that slave raiding will have been small-scale and intermittent compared to the Roman military campaigns of later date, it nonetheless could have profound demographic consequences due to its enduring recurrence.[27]

---

[24] In this role, Kessel-Lith may be compared to the Ha D-LT A fortified sites of the Scheldt River system (e.g. Kemmelberg, Kesselberg, Kester, and Kooigem) that were ideally situated to access nearby coastal regions where slaves were likely sourced.
[25] See note 45.
[26] It is during the subsequent LT B period that chariots were first deposited in burials for an even shorter period (one or two generations) across the English Channel in Yorkshire (Jay *et al.* 2012).
[27] That ancient writers not infrequently complained about slave traders draining parts of the Roman Empire of people is equally illustrative (Silver 2011: 112).

From LIA transshipment sites like Kessel-Lith, slavers and their captives likely followed river routes to the nearest *oppidum* settlements (e.g. Titelberg, Donnersberg, and Martberg). The fact that much of the evidence for metal restraints (shackles, neck rings, and chains) derives from *oppida* contexts is probably no coincidence (Schönfelder 2015; Thompson 1993). Some of these settlements contained central open spaces that are commonly interpreted as places of assembly (*area sacra*) where members of (sub-)ethnic communities are believed to have gathered for religious ceremonies, political decision-making, and commercial activity.[28] Yet, with the interests of slavers in mind, it is possible to reconsider the function of certain structural features that have been discovered at places like Titelberg, Gournay-sur-Aronde, and Villeneuve-Saint-Germain (Vandemoortele 2011: 220). What are described as 'parallel movable palisades' (Fernández-Götz 2014a: 113) are currently believed to have functioned as voting installations. However, these could also have been used to corral captives. Intriguingly, a large structure subsequently built in the location of these installations at pre-Roman Titelberg actually resembles a Roman market place (*basilica*), and it has been suggested that Mediterranean merchants maintained a trading post there (Fernández-Götz 2014c: 148, 240). That evidence for human sacrifice has also been found at Titelberg and Gournay-sur-Aronde seems as pertinent as the attested butchering and consumption of large numbers of cattle. For those communities that were involved in a trade in 'human cattle', rural cult sites or *oppidum*-based sanctuaries will have been the places where some captives were ritually killed (mostly adult men) and women and children were gathered, guarded, and cared for before being transported to faraway destinations. Their appropriated livestock, in turn, was redistributed by leaders, or collectively consumed during celebratory events that marked the completion of successful raiding campaigns. Of course, open spaces like this were likely multi-functional, allowing for a range of activities to take place. What archaeologists need to consider contextually, then, is the likelihood of places of communal assembly and ritual ceremony being used for activities organized by traders in human captives.

Following this line of inquiry, we might also look elsewhere in the study area for sites with a potential trans-shipment function. One particular site category that could have served the needs of slavers has elements in common with both the trans-Rhenian walled enclosures and the river-side trans-shipment sites described above. What are commonly referred to as 'rectilinear enclosures' have been found in substantial numbers in SW Germany (*viereckschanzen*), NW France (*enceinte carrées*), and the Scheldt-Meuse region (*cultusplaatsen*)[29] though comparable structures have been discovered across a broad swath of West-Central Europe (Berghausen 2013; Fernández-Götz 2014a: 112; Fernández-Götz and Roymans 2015; de Leeuwe and Jansen 2018; Murray 1995, 2004; von Nicolai 2006, 2009). All date to the LIA. Interpretations of their function range from the sacred, to the profane, to combinations thereof. Difficulties in interpretation no doubt result from the diversity of features discovered inside and outside many of these enclosures (deep shafts, freestanding posts, post-built structures with or without portico, hearths, and annexes). Furthermore, the associated material culture tends to be quite heterogeneous (metal tools and weapons, coins, jewelry, votive sculptures, faunal and human remains), while there is also substantial variability in landscape setting. Some enclosures had a very short use life, while others were used recurrently for extended periods of time. Regional differences have also been noted, with French *enceinte carrées* showing greater variation in morphology, material culture, and date range, and German *viereckschanzen* generally larger in size and lacking the structured depositions of their French counterparts. Yet, that this kind of site shares many characteristics cannot be denied, and these are worth listing. All were constructed with a characteristic rectilinear ditch-and-bank approach, whereby many banks were topped by a palisade perimeter. All have a single entrance that commonly show the

---

[28] If these open spaces at Treveran *oppida* mainly functioned as places of communal assembly (Fernández-Götz 2014c: 206), the absence of such public spaces in the *oppida* of other communities like the neighboring Mediomatrici remains puzzling.
[29] See note 59.

remains of causeways and/or gatehouses. Clearly, the main function of rectilinear enclosures was to restrict access to and from an enclosed space, but because the structural features that characterize this type of site were not very effective for defensive purposes, it is likely that they mainly functioned to keep whatever was kept inside from getting out. Because most enclosures contain wells or were built near springs, water provision seems to have been an important concern. This makes it possible that humans were the main occupants.

Compared to the evidence from nearby settlements, the archaeological material derived from enclosures tends to be scarce. Yet, it is worth looking at to see whether a role in the slave trade may be proposed. Where pottery analysis has taken place it is clear that coarse ware represents the largest find category, with fine wares present in small quantities only (Murray 1995: 131). This contrasts notably with ratios typical for settlement contexts. Functional analysis furthermore indicates that we are mostly dealing with larger cooking vessels, while smaller bowls and basins will have been used for serving and eating. The predominance of coarse cooking pots and eating bowls/basins (large storage vessels and small drinking vessels like cups and beakers are rare) suggests a focus on the preparation and consumption of simple meals. Furthermore, spatial analysis at the enclosure of Tomerdingen (Baden-Württemberg, Germany) has shown that the activities taking place around the gatehouse were rather different from those in the interior. The gatehouse area contained the greatest density of ceramic material (Murray 1995: 134), while also providing the highest rates of fine wares and cooking vessels. By contrast, higher proportions of serving bowls were collected in the interior of the enclosure. If these enclosures were indeed used as holding facilities for slaves, a series of scenarios can be proposed that fit the available data. With captives confined to the interior, away from the fortified boundaries that were under guard, food was either prepared at the gatehouse or was brought there from external preparation sites. Right inside the gatehouse, a feeding station was located where food was distributed to slaves who consumed it individually using coarse ware bowls, or in small groups using larger bowls/basins. Their captors remained near the gatehouse where meals were consumed using a different range of wares. Furthermore, because faunal remains are predominantly found near the gatehouse, it is likely that slavers occasionally dined on meat while their captives were fed a simple plant-based diet.

The fact that most rectilinear enclosures were used intermittently can also be understood with the interest of slavers in mind. It must be remembered that for societies constrained by transport and communication limits, seasonal long-distance trade was characterized by alternating periods of high and low activity. Even if slaves were transported to points of exchange during a predetermined time of the year, facilities had to allow for the prolonged confinement and care of captives because the itineraries of slavers will rarely have aligned perfectly. The attested intermittent use of some rectilinear enclosures suggests that there may have been a seasonal rhythm at play. Another aspect to consider is that many enclosures were located in proximity to funerary monuments or cemeteries, while the material culture from both contexts tends to diverge. Though it remains possible that enclosures facilitated communal feasting events near the resting place of ancestors, this proximity of contexts yet divergence of material culture also makes sense if rectilinear enclosures were used to house transitory convoys of 'socially dead' individuals (Patterson 1982), because these sites will have been treated as liminal spaces beyond the sphere of everyday life. Such an interpretation also suggests itself for many enclosures that were not situated in proximity to mortuary sites, but still removed from rural settlements. The presumed sacred character of some structural features found within enclosures can likewise be reassessed. For example, wood-lined shafts may have served as wells that supplied captives with drinking water, or, alternately, these could have functioned as latrines. Structures situated in the interior may have facilitated a range of mercantile activity, while these could also quarter vulnerable or high-value captives. Individual wooden posts that are sometimes found within the interior of enclosures may have been used to place individuals on display;[30] that chaining could have occurred is suggested by the discovery of keys and chains at some enclosures (Neth and Schatz 1996: 136). The presence of dress items like bracelets, brooches, and neck rings, lastly, may point to slave beautification practices.

Moving beyond such practical considerations, it is also worth looking at ideological aspects. Iconographic evidence that might allow speculating about symbolic meaning is rarely found among enclosure assemblages, but some intriguing figural pieces were discovered at Fellbach-Schmiden (Baden-Württemberg, Germany) (Arnold 2010: 197; Nicolai 2009: 258). One item depicts a seated female figure flanked by two goats, while two other pieces show a male figure wearing a torc flanked by two goats and two stags respectively. In all cases, the figures wrap their arms protectively (or possessively) around the animals. In a recent discussion on transcultural formations, I proposed that Greek and Roman literary and representational evidence can be used to suggest that slaving groups contributed to Apollonian discourse, 'a transcultural formation of mytho-historical constructs, elements of which were negotiated by widely distributed groups and individuals as understandings permitted, interests encouraged, or circumstances demanded' (2017a: 11). The position I take is that discursive constructs known from Greco-Roman sources can aid the interpretation of symbolic expressions found among neighboring populations because no cultural formation ever forms in isolation. The main challenge to overcome, then, is unravelling entanglements of mytho-historical constructs that are always expressed through a wide range of media and practices, and by actors with various social and cultural backgrounds, and situated motivations. While LIA interactions between Gallic and Italic agents shaped distinct Gallo-Roman constructs, it is likely that Greek merchants arriving through Saône and Danube trade routes had contributed to earlier formations. Even though a cautious view holds that the occurrence of Greek material culture in trans-Alpine Europe by itself does not signify the actual presence there of Greek actors, other forms of evidence seem to point in that direction.[31] A possible symbolic meaning for the Fellbach-Schmiden figures may be suggested, then, by considering Greek and Roman sources. The representation of goats may have referenced a well-known mythological narrative, namely that of the Titaness Rhea hiding her son Zeus from her brother/husband Cronus. While in hiding, the infant Zeus was nursed by the she-Goat Amalthea. Possibly, the male depicted here is Zeus embracing the kids (*haedi*) of his foster-mother. In Greek astronomical tradition (Hyginus *On Astronomy* II.13) Amalthea and her two kids formed the constellation *Capra* (female goat), though in Roman times (Ptolemy *Almagest* VII 1.9) they were included with the constellation *Aurigae* (the charioteer). In the northern hemisphere, this constellation is visible throughout the year and includes one of the sixth brightest stars (*Capella*, little goat), making it a prime candidate for having been used for celestial navigation and calendrical calculations. If rectilinear enclosures served as places where merchants of various origins could meet during a particular time of year, shared use of a celestial calendar would also have been hugely beneficial for matching itineraries.[32]

Yet, because various beliefs and practices likely intersected at enclosures as nodal points in international trade circuits, multivalent expressions should be expected (Mata 2013: 136). Thus, it may have been

---

[30] See note 69.
[31] The presence of mudbrick fortifications at the EIA Heuneburg hillfort likely points to more than mere knowledge of Mediterranean construction techniques (Arnold 2010). Further, inscriptions in the Greek alphabet occur in trans-Alpine Europe from the late third century BC onwards, like those on pot sherds found at the LIA Manching *oppidum* in Bavaria, Germany (Wells 2012: 67). For the Late Republican period, we have Caesar's observation that Gallic druids used Greek writing in all 'their public and private accounts' (*Gallic Wars* VI.14). Tacitus (*Germany* I.3) later reported on a local belief that Roman Asciburgium (Moers-Asberg, Germany), situated on the west bank of the middle Rhine, was founded by the Greek Odysseus (Roman Ulysses), and that monuments and tombs inscribed with Greek writing could be found throughout southern Germany.
[32] That practices relating to astronomical observation indeed took place at some enclosures becomes more likely when they are positioned in alignment with the four cardinal points, or are known to have contained distinct series of free-standing posts that could have been used for sighting astronomical reference points.

meaningful to some profit-seeking merchants that it was Amalthea who was believed to have supplied Zeus with the horn of plenty (*cornucopia*). Further, for slavers conducting raiding expeditions into northern catchment areas, it may have been significant that Zeus' shield (*aegis*) was believed to have been fashioned from Amalthea's hide to offer the god protection in his battles with the Titans. Equally possible, I think, is Apollo and Artemis having received cultic devotion among those with commercial interests in temperate Europe because both were perceived as protectors of northern regions (Mata 2017a: 20).[33] Artemis/Diana specifically was widely regarded as protectress of girls and women, with hares, deer, and goats holding clear symbolic prominence in associated narratives and rituals. Crucially, both Apollo and Artemis/Diana were long associated with slavery in the Greco-Roman world; runaway slaves commonly sought refuge in sanctuaries dedicated to either deity, while both are regularly mentioned in the sources in connection to slave manumission rites.[34] Thus, the presence of figural depictions of goats and deer at the enclosure at Fellbach-Schmiden may relate to cultic activity focused on Artemis/Diana, and participated in by those active in the slave trade. Intriguingly, Roman-period dedications to Diana and Apollo concentrate primarily in southwest Germany (Baden-Württemberg, Bavaria, and Rhineland-Palatinate), where the highest occurrences of dedications to Diana Abnoba, Diana Sirona, and Apollo Grannus overlaps with the densest distribution of rectilinear enclosures.

I will close this multi-thread analysis of Iron Age slaving and enslavement in Northwest Europe with one final line of inquiry aimed at demonstrating the presence of slaves at a particular locality in the study area. As I suggested at the start of this book, because slavery is best approached as a complex and multifarious phenomenon, archaeologists have to move beyond searching for material 'markers' of slavery and instead examine local particularities against a background of broader historical dynamics. Such an effort makes for more convincing arguments when trying to determine the presence of slaves at any particular time and place. There are several reasons for this. To start, it is unlikely that archaeologists will ever agree on what constitutes positive material proof for the presence of slaves.[35] Further, even if acceptance of certain types of identifiers became more widespread, doubt could still be raised about the socio-cultural significance of slavery (Kusimba 2015: 247), about the transformative impact of slaving and enslavement on the developmental trajectory of a society. Lastly, it is highly likely that slaves or other kinds of subservient individuals (largely a semantic issue) have no doubt already been encountered in the archaeological record but have remained unrecognized as such.

This may indeed have been the case at the LIA Titelberg *oppidum*. Excavations at a nearby cemetery have attested a child interment rate of thirty percent (Fernández-Götz 2014c: 196). This deviates radically from a very common underrepresentation of children in mortuary contexts. It is worth asking, then, why such an abnormally high number of children was buried outside the most prominent of the

---

[33] Regarding imaginaries about the North and its inhabitants, the fact that entry-ways to rectilinear enclosures are never situated on a north side may have symbolic significance if captives were predominantly sourced from northern regions.

[34] For example, at the temple of Artemis at Ephesus (Turkey), the very site where Amazonian women pursued by Herakles were believed to have found refuge, runaway slaves were offered refuge from persecution. In Italy, meanwhile, the oldest temple on Rome's Aventine hill was devoted to Diana and its initial dedication occurred during the reign of Servius Tullius (575-535 BC) when an annual festival (*dies servorum*) was initiated and primarily participated in by women and slaves. Furthermore, the priesthood at the sanctuary of Diana at Aricia (Lake Nemi, Italy) was believed to have been occupied by runaway slaves only (Pausanias *Description of Greece* II.27.4). It may furthermore be significant that it was precisely on the Greek island of Delos, birthplace of Apollo and Artemis, where one of the largest slave markets known in Antiquity developed; there, slave trading intensified greatly during the Late Republican period (Strabo *Geography* 14.5.2).

[35] For some, objects like metal shackles are a convincing indicator for enslavement, while others argue more cautiously that such objects might also have been used to restrain prisoners of war or criminals. Further, deviant burial practices are commonly seen as evidence for low social status or poverty, and not directly linked to enslavement, let alone institutionalized slavery. Reversely, grave goods like dress items are commonly treated as indicators for high social status or economic wealth, while this could equally be used to argue for slave beautification practices. Because of such difficulties alone, contextual, relational, and comparative analyses are key.

Treveran hillforts. It may well have been the case that a magnified concern for children arose in parts of the study area, particularly among groups where family autonomy and distinction gained ideological importance. Within such communities we can expect certain practices and expressions (e.g. special mortuary treatment, sacred rituals) relating to child welfare to manifest. That this happened among both the Treveri and the Batavi is suggested by votive dedications to Mars/Mercurius Iovantucarus (guardian of the young) and Hercules Magusanus (old youth) that were made to secure the wellbeing of children (Roymans 1990, 57). Yet, paradoxically, we may also expect similar concerns to arise among groups that traded in child captives or exploited children for their labor, in which case practices and expressions were more likely focused on productivity or the successful completion of risky but profitable ventures. It is worth considering whether children were systematically exploited for their labor at this prominent Treveran settlement, because it strikes me as inconceivable that the attested expansion of industrial-scale manufacturing across the West-Central European *oppidum* zone (Wells 2002: 369) did not coincide with a rise in the exploitation of slave labor.[36] At the Titelberg settlement it is the deviant child interment rate especially that encourages speculating about the exploitation of child labor.

The concept of child labor is of course very much shaped by modern ideals of child development. Children have always labored alongside adults, and many across the globe still do (André and Godin 2013; Watson 2018). It was no different in the Greco-Roman world, where only the children of wealthy citizens had a chance of enjoying a childhood free of labor (Laes 2011). Yet, a distinction has to be maintained between the contributions that children have always made to the reproduction of their families and communities on the one hand, and the forced and purposeful use of child labor by unscrupulous exploiters on the other (Campbell *et al.* 2009).[37] If it can be accepted that the Titelberg *oppidum* had an important commercial function for slave traders, this urges gauging the likelihood of forced labor having been exploited there.

Children can be quite adept at specific labor tasks. For instance, they have historically been used in mining (small bodies in confined spaces), as well as small metal craft (small nimble fingers and good eye-sight).[38] It seems significant, then, that the Treveran *oppidum* is known to have been a prolific producer of small metal objects and that iron ore was mined in the area during the LIA. The mint foundries at this settlement seem to have been particularly productive (Rowlett 1988).[39] However, in the Rhine-Moselle region it is textile manufacture which has the greatest potential for having relied on child labor. While the production of woolen fabrics was an important industry in the Treveran area during the Roman period, this particular domain of economic activity was initially established during the LIA (Drinkwater 1982). One critical point to consider here is that urbanization and social stratification historically have

---

[36] Indeed, while the clearest evidence for slave-based manufacturing stems from the Mediterranean world, forcing people to partake in large-scale production efforts – like private pottery or state-run textile workshops – certainly was not a Roman innovation. See Kristiansen (1998: 116), who suggests that slaves may have been exploited in mining in Central Europe during the LIA.

[37] For comparison, see Sîrbu (2008) on the interment of children among the Geto-Dacians, which occurred intermittently over the course of the 4th-2nd centuries BC, but peaked during the 1st centuries BC and AD. Notably, traditional burial practices declined starting in the late 3rd century BC. From then onwards, the manner in which children were buried varied significantly, with archaeologists finding great diversity in terms of location, position, orientation, and degree of skeletal articulation. Both single and multiple interments occur, and some remains show signs of violence. Grave goods, in turn, are commonly lacking. While it remains difficult to relate such heterogeneity in burial practices directly to slavery, it is noteworthy that huge numbers of Republican *denarii* arrived in the Lower Danube basin during the 2nd-1st century BC, a phenomenon that Crawford (1977) links to the slave trade.

[38] The manufacture of Bronze Age daggers may have involved child labor because the application of fine decorative details would have required excellent eye-sight (personal communication with David Dawson, director at Wiltshire Museum, UK).

[39] While the discovery of an infant burial near a bronze casting furnace has led archaeologists to suggest sacred ritual (Shaw 2007: 15), if we allow for the possibility that adolescent children were exploited for their labor a more depressing scenario suggests itself.

coincided with rising demands for cloth, likely because increased interaction with non-kin leads to a greater interest for manipulating outward appearance (Dimova 2016; Gleba 2014).[40] The commencement of (proto-)urban habitation in the southern part of the study area, where communities were linked into interregional exchange networks, is one reason to suspect that local households interested in becoming more autonomous economically and distinguished socially delegated various labor-intensive activities to slaves, including textile production. Historically, domestic and industrial cloth manufacture has commonly been allocated to slaves. Greek sources provide evidence for the use of slave labor in textile industry (Aeschines *Against Timarchus* I.97; Wild 1976: 53), as do more recent comparative sources (Schneider 1987). Notably, most textile production steps can be performed by children, such that it should not surprise us to find that children were active in textile production in the Minoan and Mycenaean palaces of the Bronze Age (Nosch 2001, 2014), as well as among Etruscan households (Nash-Briggs 2003: 253). It is not unreasonable to suggest, then, that indigenous agents active in the slave trade, those who participated in satisfying an enduring Mediterranean demand for slaves, would eventually also recognize its potential for local production efforts. It seems likely that the same processes and dynamics that initially operated across the Mediterranean world (e.g. stratification, commercialization, and urbanization), and later throughout parts of trans-Alpine Europe, would result in comparable transitions in the study area where it is among southern groups in particular that we can expect a shift from trading in slaves to trading in the productive fruits of slave labor during the LIA.

---

[40] Congruent with this growing interest for managing outward appearance is the attested LT D growth in brooch diversity and ornamentality throughout trans-Alpine Europe, a phenomenon that is particularly visible in *oppida* assemblages (Edgar 2012).

Conclusion

Well before I started writing this book I became preoccupied with a central question: if slaving and enslavement could be shown to have been significant transformative phenomena in Iron Age Europe, how would this affect the interpretation of (old and new) archaeological evidence, and how would this change ideas about broader socio-cultural developments that have long been considered known by those who have looked at these things through the lens of 'acculturation' or 'complexification'? It appears to me that there has been little interest for slavery in Iron Age Europe as a distinct topic of research, especially when compared to work done for other periods and places. This is a curious state of affairs considering the clear cross-paradigmatic recognition of competition and conflict as prime movers of historical transformation. How is it that prehistorians of temperate Europe see evidence for social stratification and inter-group conflict in so many contexts, yet grant slaving and enslavement so little attention? Arguably, a long-standing interest for distinguishing between trans-Alpine ('barbarian', 'native') and Mediterranean ('civilized', 'colonial') cultural spheres may have encouraged archaeologists of diverse theoretical persuasions to compare the systems of inequality that undoubtedly existed in both in starkly contrasting terms. While such tendencies already came to the fore in the earliest (antiquarian, culture-historical) phase of the archaeological discipline, post-processual (post-colonialist, structuralist, Marxist, interpretivist) perspectives, in particular, only seem to have reinforced these. As I argued elsewhere (Mata 2017a), it is important to recognize that cultural entanglements throughout prehistoric Europe continued for millennia, despite political ruptures, economic breakdowns, and societal collapses. Consequently, any argument that suggests stark cultural boundaries for any particular time or place has to be tested through careful consideration of historical dynamics operating at multiple (local, regional, 'global') levels of manifestation.

As I have attempted to show, for Iron Age groups in Northwest Europe it was not contact with foreign traders with general mercantile interests that triggered a supposedly dormant potential for complexification (social differentiation, political centralization); rather, it was a very specific Mediterranean demand for slaves that impacted peripheral peoples in distinct ways, triggering a variety of responses in particular localities, including an understandable interest for refuge construction and a strengthening of martial ideologies. I also emphasized the effects that social disorder, economic stress, and physical insecurity can have on human psychology and communal life. The interests, motivations, and outlooks that will have taken shape under such conditions stimulated a wide variety of behaviors and expressions that can be understood by archaeologists. But, the unraveling of such complex material, behavioral, and ideological entanglements demands taking a multi-thread approach whereby a wide range of material categories and domains of social practice are contextually and relationally examined, in reference to comparative data derived from other periods and places.

It is worth ending this preliminary contribution to the study of Iron Age slavery in Northwest Europe by again pointing out that the various trends (political centralization, social stratification, wealth accumulation) that led to greater inequality throughout the Mediterranean region were driven by a central motivation: a desire experienced by countless individuals and their kin for economic security, social recognition, and cultural belonging (Miller 2008: 75). While such basic human motivations can indeed be deemed universal, how this exhibits through particular attitudes, behaviors, and discourses is never certain. One central way in which many residents of ancient Mediterranean city-states sought to realize these aspirations was by exploiting the bodies and labor of the social and cultural *Other*, initially destitute citizens and countrymen but then increasingly enslaved foreigners. The peoples of temperate Europe were greatly impacted by these 'global' dynamics, and similar developments eventually manifested there as well. Perhaps inevitably, Mediterranean communities increasingly sought to control their barbarian sources of human labor, and this will have been a major contributing factor to rising levels of antagonism and conflict during the LIA.

References

Ancient Sources

Aeschines (Translation by C. D. Adams 1919). *Against Timachus*. London: W. Heinemann. Perseus Digital Library, last viewed 15 March 2019, <http://www.perseus.tufts.edu>.

Appian (Translation by H. White 1899). *The Civil Wars*. London: MacMillan and Co. Perseus Digital Library, last viewed 15 March 2019, <http://www.perseus.tufts.edu>.

Aristotle (Translation by G.C. Armstrong 1935). *Economics*. London: W. Heinemann. Perseus Digital Library, last viewed 15 March 2019, <http://www.perseus.tufts.edu>.

Julius Caesar (Translation by J. Warrington 1954). *The Gallic Wars*. Verona: Limited Editions Club Officina Bodoni.

Cassius Dio Cocceianus (Translation by E. Cary 1914). *Dio's Roman History*. London: W. Heinemann.

Cicero (Translation by E.S. Shuckburgh 1908-1909). *Letters to Atticus*. London: George Belle and Sons. Perseus Digital Library, last viewed 15 March 2019, <http://www.perseus.tufts.edu>.

Diodorus Siculus (Translation by C.H. Oldfather 1989). *Library of History*. London: W. Heinemann. Perseus Digital Library, last viewed 15 March 2019, <http://www.perseus.tufts.edu>.

Faḍlān, A. Ibn (Translation by P. Lunde and C. Stone 2012). *Ibn Fadlan and the Land of Darkness: Arab Travellers in the Far North*. London: Penguin.

Herodotus (Translation by A.D. Godley 1920). *The Histories*. Cambridge, MA: Harvard University Press. Perseus Digital Library, last viewed 15 March 2019, <http://www.perseus.tufts.edu>.

Hyginus (Translation by M. Grant 1960). *On Astronomy*. Lawrence: University of Kansas Publications. Theoi Classical Texts Library, last viewed 15 March 2019, <https://www.theoi.com>.

Orosius (Translation A. T. Fear 2010). *Seven Books of History against the Pagans*. Liverpool: Liverpool University Press.

Ovid (Translation by T. Bishop 2003). *Amores*. Manchester: Carcanet Press Ltd.

Pausanias (Translation by W.H.S. Jones 1918). *Description of Greece*. London: W. Heinemann. Perseus Digital Library, last viewed 15 March 2019, <http://www.perseus.tufts.edu>.

Philostratus (Translation by F. C. Conybeare 1912). *Life of Apollonius of Tyana*. Cambridge: Harvard University Press. Livius. Cultuur, geschiedenis en literatuur, last viewed 15 March 2019 <https://www.livius.org>.

Pliny the Elder (Translation by J. Bostock and H.T. Riley 1855). *The Natural History*. London: Taylor and Francis. Perseus Digital Library, last viewed 15 March 2019, <http://www.perseus.tufts.edu>.

Plutarch (Translation by B. Perrin 1921). *Parallel Lives*. Cambridge: Harvard University Press. Perseus Digital Library, last viewed 15 March 2019, <http://www.perseus.tufts.edu>.

Polybius (Translation E.S. Shuckburgh 1889): *Histories*. London: Macmillan. Perseus Digital Library, last viewed 15 March 2019, <http://www.perseus.tufts.edu>.

Ptolemy (Translation by G.J. Toomer 1984): *Ptolemy's Almagest*. London: Duckworth.

Strabo (Edited by H.L. Jones 1924): *The Geography of Strabo*. London: W. Heinemann. Perseus Digital Library, last viewed 15 March 2019, <http://www.perseus.tufts.edu>.

Tacitus (A.J. Church, W.J. Brodribb, and L. Cerrato 1942): *Germany and its Tribes*. New York: Random House. Perseus Digital Library, last viewed 15 March 2019, <http://www.perseus.tufts.edu>.

Tacitus (Translation by A.J. Church, W.J. Brodribb, and S. Bryant 1873): *The History*. New York: Random House Perseus Digital Library, last viewed 15 March 2019, <http://www.perseus.tufts.edu>.

Modern Sources

Afigbo, A. E. 2006. The Abolition of the Slave Trade in Southeastern Nigeria, 1885-1950. Rochester: University of Rochester Press.

Ailincăi, S-C. 2016. Living with the Dead. Burials in Early Iron Age Settlements between the Balkans, Tisza and Dnestr, in V. Sirbu, M. Jevtić, K. Dmitrović and M. Ljuština (eds) Funerary Practices During the Bronze and Iron Ages in central and Southeast Europe. Proceedings of the 14th International Colloquium of Funerary Archaeology in Čačak, Serbia, 24th-27th September 2015: 135-164. Belgrade: University of Belgrade.

Aldhouse-Green, M. 2004. Chaining and Shaming: Images of Defeat, From Llyn Cerrig Bach to Sarmitzegetusa. Oxford Journal of Archaeology 23 (3): 319-340.

Aldhouse-Green, M. 2005: Bondage, violence, slavery and sacrifice in later European prehistory, in M. Parker-Pearson and I.J. Thorpe (eds) Warfare, violence and slavery in prehistory: proceedings of a Prehistoric Society conference at Sheffield University 2001. British Archaeological Reports 1374: 155-164. Oxford: BAR Publishing.

Alexander, J. 2001. Islam, archaeology and slavery in Africa. World Archaeology 33 (1): 44-60.

André, G. and M. Godin 2013. Child labour, agency and family dynamics: The case of mining in Katanga (DRC). Childhood 21 (2): 161-174.

Angelini, I. and P. Bellintani 2005. Archaeological Ambers from Northern Italy: an FTIR-Drift Study of Provenance by Comparison with the Geological Amber Database. Archaeometry 47 (2): 441-454.

Arnold, B. 1988. Slavery in Late Prehistoric Europe: Recovering the Evidence for Social Structure in Iron Age Society, in D.B. Gibson and M.N. Geselowitz (eds) Tribe and Polity in Late Prehistoric Europe: 179-192. New York: Plenum Press.

Arnold, B. 1999. 'Drinking the Feast': Alcohol and the Legitimation of Power in Celtic Europe. Cambridge Archaeological Journal 9 (1): 71-93.

Arnold, B. 2010. Eventful archaeology, the Heuneburg mudbrick wall, and the EIA of southwest Germany, in D.J. Bolender (ed.) Eventful Archaeologies: New Approaches to Social Transformation in the Archaeological Record: 100-114. Albany: State University of New York Press.

Arnold, B. 2011. The Illusion of Power, the Power of Illusion, in R. Bernbeck and R.H. McGuire (eds) Ideologies in Archaeology. Tucson: University of Arizona Press: 151-172.

Arnold, B. and D. B. Gibson (eds) 1995. Celtic Chiefdom, Celtic State: The Evolution of Complex Social Systems in Prehistoric Europe. Cambridge: Cambridge University Press.

Arnold, B. and M. L. Murray 2002. "Put Out the Geese, The Celts are Coming". Iron Age Migration and Social Change in Central Europe, in C. Allum, J. Kahn, C. Cluney and M. Peurakmaki-Brown (eds) Ancient Travellers: Proceedings of the Twenty-Seventh Annual Conference of the Archaeological Association of the University of Calgary: 111-118. Calgary: University of Calgary.

Arnoldussen, S. and R. Jansen 2010. Iron Age Habitation Patterns on the Southern and Northern Dutch Pleistocene Coversand Soils: The Process of Settlement Nucleation, in M. Meyer (ed.) Haus - Gehöft - Weiler - Dorf. Siedlungen der Vorrömischen Eisenzeit im nördlichen Mitteleuropa. Internationale Tagung an der Freien Universität Berlin vom 20.-22. Marz 2009. Berliner Archäologische Forschungen 8: 379-397. Berlin: Verlag Marie Leidorf.

Avram, A. 2007. Some Thoughts about the Black Sea and the Slave Trade before the Roman Domination (6th-1st Centuries BC), in V. Gabrielsen and J. Lund (eds) The Black Sea in Antiquity. Regional and Interregional Economic Exchanges. Black Sea Studies 6: 239-251. Aarhus: Aarhus University Press.

Barrett, J.C. 2012. Are Models of Prestige Goods Economies and Conspicuous Consumption Applicable to the Archaeology of the Bronze Age to Iron Age Transition in Britain?, in A. M. Jones, J. Pollard, M.J. Allen and J. Gardiner (eds) Image, Memory and Monumentality. Archaeological engagements with the material world: a celebration of the academic achievements of Professor Richard Bradley. Prehistoric Society Research paper 5: 6-17. Oxford: Oxbow Books.

Bartman, E. 2001. Hair and the Artifice of Roman Female Adornment. American Journal of Archaeology 105 (1): 1-25.

Baum, R.M. 1999. Shrines of the Slave Trade: Diola Religion and Society in Precolonial Senegambia. Oxford: Oxford University Press.

Bauman, R.A. 1992. Women and Politics in Ancient Rome. London: Routledge.

Bazelmans, J. 1999. By Weapons Made Worthy: Lords, Retainers, and Their Relationship in Beowulf. Amsterdam Archaeological Studies 5. Amsterdam: Amsterdam University Press.

Beauvoir, S. de 1968. The Second Sex. New York: Modern Library.

Benelli, E. 2013. Slavery and Manumission, in J.M. Turfa (ed.) The Etruscan World. New York: Routledge: 447-456.

Berghausen, K. 2013. Magnetometrische Untersuchungen an spätkeltischen Viereckschanzen in Bayern. Unpublished PhD Dissertation, Geology, Ludwig-Maximilian University Munich.

Berlin, I. 1998. Many Thousands Gone: The First Two Centuries of Slavery in North America. Cambridge: Harvard University Press.

Bloemers, J.H.F. 1986. A cart burial from a small Middle Iron cemetery in Nijmegen, in M. van Bakel, R.R. Hagesteijn and P. van de Velde (eds) Private politics. A multi-disciplinary approach to 'Big Man' systems: 76-95. Leiden: Brill.

Blundell, S. 1995. Women in Ancient Greece. Cambridge: Harvard University Press.

Bodel, J. 2005. Caveat emptor: towards a study of Roman slave-traders. Journal of Roman Archaeology 18. 181-195.

Bourdieu, P. 1977. Outline of a Theory of Practice. Cambridge: Cambridge University Press.

Bourgeois, Q. and S. van der Vaart-Verschoof 2017. A practice perspective: understanding Early Iron Age elite burials in the southern Netherlands through event-based analysis, in R. Schumann and S. van der Vaart-Verschoof (eds) Connecting Elites and Regions. Perspectives on contacts, relations and differentiation during the Early Iron Age Hallstatt C period in Northwest and Central Europe: 305-318. Leiden: Sidestone Press.

Bradley, K. 1992. "The Regular, Daily Traffic in Slaves": Roman History and Contemporary History. The Classical Journal 87 (2): 125-138.

Bradley, K. 2000. Animalizing the Slave: The Truth of Fiction. Journal of Roman Studies 90: 110-125.

Bradley, R. and K. Gordon 1988. Human skulls from the river Thames, their dating and significance. Antiquity 62: 503-509.

Braund, D.C. and G.R. Tsetskhladze 1989. The Export of Slaves from Colchis. The Classical Quarterly. New Series 39 (1): 114-125.

Broeke, P.W. van den 2014. Inhumation Burials: New Elements in iron Age Funerary Ritual in the Southern Netherlands, in A. Cahen-Delhaye and G. de Mulder (eds) Des Espaces aux Esprits. L'organisation de la mort aux âges de Métaux dans le nord-oest de l'Europe. Études et Documents Archéologie 32: 161-184. Namur: Institut du Patrimoine Wallon.

Brun, P. 1994. From the Hallstatt to La Tène Period in the Perspective of the Mediterranean World economy, in K. Kristiansen and J. Jensen (eds) Europe in the First Millenium B.C. Sheffield Archaeological Monographs 6: 57-66. Sheffield: J.R. Collis Publications.

Brun, P. 1995. Oppida and Social 'complexification' in France, in J.D. Hill and C.G. Cumberpatch (eds) Different Iron Ages. Studies on the Iron Age in temperate Europe. British Archaeological Reports International Series 602: 121-128. Oxford: BAR Publishing.

Cameron, C.M. 2008. Introduction: Captives in Prehistory as Agents of Social Change, in C.M. Cameron (ed.) Invisible Citizens: Captives and Their Consequences: 1-24. Salt Lake City: University of Utah Press.

Cameron, C.M. 2011. Captives and Culture Change Implications for Archaeology. Current Anthropology 52 (2): 169-209.

Cameron, C.M. and D.L. Martin 2012. Archaeological and Bioarchaeological Perspectives on Captivity and Slavery. Anthropology News 53 (7): 4-5.

Campbell, G., S. Miers and J.C. Miller (eds) 2009. Children in Slavery through the Ages. Athens: Ohio University Press.

Certeau, M. de 1988. The Practice of Everyday Life. Berkeley: University of California Press.

Collis, J.R. 1975. Defended Sites of the Late La Tène in Central and Western Europe. British Archaeological Reports International Series 2. Oxford: BAR Publishing.

Collis, J.R. 1977. Pre-Roman Burial Rites in North-Western Europe, in R. Reece (ed.) Burial in the Roman World: 1-13. London: Council for British Archaeology.

Collis, J.R. 1984. Oppida: earliest towns north of the Alps. Sheffield: University of Sheffield.

Conteh-Morgan, E. 2002. Globalization and Human Security: A Neo-Gramscian Perspective. International Journal of Peace Studies 7 (2): 57-73.

Cosack, E. and P. Kehne 1999. Ein archäologisches Zeugnis zum germanisch-römischen Sklavenhandel? Römisch-Germanisches Zentralmuseum. Archäologisches Korrespondenzblatt 29: 97-109.

Crawford, M.H. 1977. Republican Denarii in Romania: The Suppression of Piracy and the Slave-Trade. Journal of Roman Studies 67: 117-124.

Creighton, J. 2000. Coins and Power in Late Iron Age Britain. New Studies in Archaeology. Cambridge:
Cambridge University Press.

Cunliffe, B.W. 1997. The Ancient Celts. Oxford: Oxford University Press.

Curto, J.C. 2004. Enslaving Spirits: The Portuguese-Brazilian Alcohol Trade at Luanda and Its Hinterland, c. 1550-1830. Leiden: Brill.

Czebreszuk, J. 2003. Amber on the Threshold of a World Career, in C.W. Beck, I.B. Loze and J.M. Todd (eds) Amber in Archaeology. Proceedings of the Fourth International Conference on Amber in Archaeology, Talsi 2001. International Union of prehistoric and Protohistoric Sciences. Amber Committee, Association for the Advancement of Baltic Studies: 164-179. Riga: Institute of the History of Latvia Publishers.

Czebreszuk, J. 2007. Amber between the Baltic and the Aegean in the Third and Second Millenia BC (an outline of major issues), in I. Galanaki, H. Tomas, Y. Galanakis and R. Laffineur (eds) Between the Aegean and Baltic Seas. Prehistory across Borders. Proceedings of the International Conference Bronze and Early Iron Age Interconnections and Contemporary Developments between the Aegean and the Regions of the Balkan Peninsula, Central and Northern Europe. University of Zagreb, 11-14 April 2005. Aegaeum 27: 363-370. Liège: Université de Liège.

Dal Lago, E. and C. Katsari (eds) 2008. Slave Systems: Ancient and Modern. Cambridge: Cambridge University Press.

Dalton, J.T. and T.C. Leung 2011. Why is Polygyny More Prevalent in Western Africa? An African Slave Trade Perspective. Working Paper. Munich Personal RePEc Archive. Munich: Munich University.

Daubigney, A. and J.-P. Guillaumet 1985. L'entrave de Glanon (Côte d'Or), les Eduens et l'esclavage, in Bonnamour, L. A., Duval, and J.-P. Guillaumet (eds) Les Âges du Fer dans la vallée de la Saône (VIIe-Ier siècles avant notre ère): Paléométallurgie du bronze à l'Âge du Fer. Actes du septième colloque de l'A.F.E.A.F. tenu à Rully, 12-15 mai 1983. Revue Archéologique de l'Est et Centre-Est (6e suppl.): 171-177.

DeBoer, W.R. 2008. Wrenched Bodies, in C.M. Cameron (ed.) Invisible Citizens: Captives and Their Consequences: 233-261. Salt Lake City: University of Utah Press.

Derks, T. 1998. Gods, Temples, and Ritual Practices: The Transformation of Religious Ideas and Values in Roman Gaul. Amsterdam Archaeological Studies. Amsterdam: Amsterdam University Press.

Díaz-Andreu, M and T. Champion (eds) 1996. Nationalism and Archaeology in Europe. London: Routledge.

Diepeveen-Jansen, M. 2001. People, Ideas and Goods: New Perspectives on 'Celtic Barbarians' in Western and Central Europe (500-250 BC). Amsterdam: Amsterdam University Press.

Dietler, M. 1989. Greeks, Etruscans and thirsty barbarians: Early Iron Age interaction in the Rhône basin of France, in T. Champion (ed.) Centre and Periphery: Comparative Studies in Archaeology: 127-141. London: Unwin Hyman.

Dietler, M. 1990. Driven by Drink: The Role of Drinking in the Political Economy and the Case of Early Iron Age France. Journal of Anthropological Archaeology 9: 352-406.

Dietler, M. 1994. "Our Ancestors the Gauls": Archaeology, Ethnic Nationalism, and the Manipulation of Celtic Identity in Modern Europe. American Anthropologist New Series 96 (3): 584-605.

Dietler, M. 1995. Early "Celtic" socio-political relations: ideological representation and social competition in dynamic comparative perspective, B. Arnold and D.B. Gibson (eds) Celtic chiefdom, Celtic state. The evolution of complex social systems in prehistoric Europe: 64-71. Cambridge: Cambridge University Press.

Dietler, M. 2006. Alcohol: anthropological/archaeological perspectives. Annual Review of Anthropology 35: 229-249.

Dietler, M. 2010. Archaeologies of Colonialism: Consumption, Entanglement, and Violence in Ancient Mediterranean France. Berkeley: University of California Press.

Dietler, M. and I. Herbich 2001. Feasts and Labor Mobilization: Dissecting a Fundamental Economic Practice, in M. Dietler and B. Hayden (eds) Feasts: Archaeological and Ethnographic Perspectives on Food, Politics, and Power. Smithsonian Series in Archaeological Inquiry: 240-264. Washington D.C.: Smithsonian Institution Press

Dimova, B. 2016. Textile Production in Iron Age Thrace. European Journal of Archaeology 19 (4): 652-680.

Dornan, J.L. 2002. Agency and Archaeology: Past, Present and Future Directions. Journal of Archaeological Method and Theory 9 (4): 303–29.

Drinkwater, J.F. 1982. The Wool Textile Industry of Gallia Belgica and the Secundinii of Igel: Questions and Hypotheses. Textile History 12 (1): 111-28.

Eckardt, H. and N. Crummy 2008. Styling the body in Late Iron Age and Roman Britain: a contextual approach to toilet instruments. Monographies Instrumentum 36. Dremil-Lafage: Éditions Mergoil.

Edgar, M. 2012. Beyond Typology: Late Iron Age and Early Roman Brooches in Northern France. Unpublished PhD Dissertation, Archaeology and Ancient History, University of Leicester.

Egg, M. 2017. The Iron Age Cremation Cemetery of Wörgl in Tyrol and the Early Hallstatt Mindelheim Horizon, in R. Schumann and S. van der Vaart-Verschoof (eds) Connecting Elites and Regions: Perspectives on Contacts, Relations and Differentiation during the Early Iron Age Hallstatt C Period in Northwest and Central Europe: 49-65. Leiden: Sidestone Press.

Erchak, G.M. 1992. The Anthropology of Self and Behavior. New Brunswick: Rutgers University Press.

Fentress, E.W.B. 2011. Slavers on chariots, in A. Dowler and E.R. Galvin (eds) Money, Trade and Trade Routes in Pre-Islamic North Africa. British Museum Research Publication 176: 65-71. London: British Museum.

Fernández-Götz, M. 2014a. Sanctuaries and Ancestor Worship at the Origin of the Oppida, in V. Sirbu and S. Matei (eds) Residential Centres (dava, emporium, oppidum, hillfort, polis) and Cult Places in the Second Iron Age of Europe. Mousaios 19: 111-132. Buzău: Muzeul Judetean Buzău.

Fernández-Götz, M. 2014b. Central Places and the Construction of Collective Identities in the Middle Rhine-Moselle Region, in C. N. Popa and S. Stoddart (eds) Fingerprinting the Iron Age. Approaches to Identity in the European Iron Age. Integrating South-Eastern Europe into the Debate: 175-186. Oxford: Oxbow Books.

Fernández-Götz, M. 2014c. Identity and Power. The Transformation of Iron Age Societies in Northeast Gaul. Amsterdam: Amsterdam University Press.

Fernández-Götz, M. 2016. Revisiting Migrations in Archaeology: The Aisne-Marne and the Hunsrück-Eifel Cultures, in G. Erskine JR, P. Jacobsson, P. Miller, and S. Stetkiewicz (eds) Proceedings of the 17th Iron Age Research Student Symposium, Edinburgh 29th May - 1st June 2014: 1-11. Oxford: Archaeopress.

Fernández-Götz, M. 2018. Urbanization in Iron Age Europe: Trajectories, Patterns, and Social Dynamics. Journal of Archaeological Research 26: 117-162.

Fernández-Götz, M. and D. Krausse 2013. Rethinking Early Iron Age urbanization in Central Europe: the Heuneburg site and its archaeological environment. Antiquity 87: 473-487.

Fernández-Götz, M., H. Wendling and K. Winger (eds) 2014. Paths to Complexity: Centralisation and Urbanisation in Iron Age Europe. Oxford: Oxbow Books.

Fernández-Götz, M. and I. Ralston 2017. The Complexity and Fragility of Early Iron Age Urbanism in West-Central Temperate Europe. Journal of World Prehistory 30: 259-279.

Fernández-Götz, M. and N. Roymans 2015. The Politics of Identity: Late Iron Age Sanctuaries in the Rhineland, in A. Sanmark, F. Iversen, N. Mehler and S. Semple (eds) Debating the Thing in the North II: Selected Papers from Workshops Organized by The Assembly Project. Journal of the North Atlantic Special Volume 8: 18-32. Steuben: Eagle Hill Publications.

Fernández-Götz, M. and B. Arnold 2017. Elites before the Fürstensitze, in R. Schumann and S. van der Vaart-Verschoof (eds) Connecting Elites and Regions: Perspectives on Contacts, Relations and Differentiation during the Early Iron Age Hallstatt C Period in Northwest and Central Europe: 183-199. Leiden: Sidestone Press.

Fiedler, S., U. Veit and J. Wahl 2009. Menschliche Skelettreste aus der eisenzeitlichen Höhensiedlung auf der Achalm, Stadt Reutlingen - Archäologischer Befund und anthropologische Untersuchungen. Fundberichte Aus Baden-Württemberg 30: 95-123.

Finley, M.I. 1959. Was Greek Civilization Based on Slave labour? Historia: Zeitschrift für Alte Geschichte 8 (2): 145-164.

Finley, M.I. 1962. The Slave Trade in Antiquity: the Black Sea and Danubian regions. Klio 40: 51-59.

Finley, M.I. 1980. Ancient Slavery and Modern Ideology. New York: Penguin Books.

Fitts, M.E. 2015. The Indian Slave Trade and Catawba History, in L.W. Marshall (ed.) The Archaeology of Slavery: A Comparative Approach to Captivity and Coercion. Center for Archaeological Investigations Southern Illinois University Carbondale Occasional Paper 41: 300-325. Carbondale: Southern Illinois University Press.

Fokkens, H. 1998. Drowned Landscape: The Occupation of the Western Part of the Frisian-Drentian Plateau, 4400 BC-AD 500. Assen: Van Gorcum.

Fokkens, H., S.A. van der Vaart, D.R. Fontijn, S.A.M. Lemmers, R. Jansen, I.M. van Wijk and P.J.C. Valentijn 2012. Hallstatt burials of Oss in context, in C. Bakels and H. Kamermans (eds) The End of Our Fifth Decade. Analecta Praehistorica Leidensia 43/44: 183-204. Leiden: Leiden University.

Fontaine, J.M. 2017. Slave Trading in the British Isles and the Czech Lands, 7th-11th Centuries. Unpublished PhD Dissertation, History, King's College London.

Fontijn, D. and H. Fokkens 2007. The emergence of Early Iron Age 'chieftains' graves' in the southern Netherlands: reconsidering transformations in burial and depositional practices, in C. Haselgrove and R. Pope (eds) The earlier Iron Age in Britain and the Near Continent: 354-373. Oxford: Oxbow Books.

Frankenstein, S. and Rowlands, M. 1978. The internal structure and regional context of Early Iron Age society in south-western Germany. Bulletin of the Institute of Archaeology London 15: 73-112. London: Institute of Archaeology.

Gavriljuk, N. A. 2003. The Graeco-Scythian Slavetrade in the 6th and 5th Centuries BC, in G. Bilde, J. Munk Højte and V. F. Stolba (eds) The Cauldron of Ariantas. Danish National Research Foundation's Centre for Black Sea Studies 1: 75-85. Aarhus: Aarhus University Press.

Gerritsen, F.A. 2003. Local Identities: Landscape and Community in the Late Prehistoric Meuse-Demer-Scheldt Region. Amsterdam Archaeological Studies 9. Amsterdam: Amsterdam University Press.

Gerritsen, F.A. and N. Roymans 2006. Central Places and the Construction of Tribal Identities. The Case of the Late Iron Age Lower Rhine Region, in Haselgrove (ed.) Celtes et Gaulois l'archéologie face a l'histoire. Les mutations de la fin de l'Âge du fer. Actes de la table ronde de Cambridge, 7-8 juillet 2005. Collection Bribracte 12/4: 251-266. Glux-en-Glenne: Centre Archéologique Européen.

Gijn, A.L. van, and H.T. Waterbolk 1984. The Colonization of the Salt Marshes of Friesland and Groningen: The Possibility of a Transhumant Prelude. Palaeohistoria 26: 101-122.

Giddens, A. 1984. The Constitution of Society: Outline of the Theory of Structuration. Berkeley: University of California Press.

Giumlia-Mair, A.R. and F. Lo Schiavo (eds) 2003. The Problem of Early Tin. British Archaeological Reports International Series 1199. Oxford: BAR Publishing.

Gleba, M. 2014. The Fabric for a City: Development of Textile Materials during the Urbanization Period in Mediterranean Europe. Textile Society of America 2014 Biennial Symposium Proceedings: New Directions: Examining the Past, Creating the Future, Los Angeles, California, September 10-14, 2014: 1-9. Lincoln: University of Nebraska.

González-Ruibal, A. 2012. Archaeology and the Study of Material Culture: Synergies with Cultural Psychology, in J. Vaalsiner (ed.) Oxford Handbook of Cultural Psychology: 132-162. New York: Oxford University Press.

Graham, J.D. 1965. The Slave Trade, Depopulation and Human Sacrifice in Benin History. Cahiers d'Études Africaines 5 (18): 317-334.

Gronenborn, D. 2001. Zum (möglichen) Nachweis von Sklaven/Unfreien in prähistorischen Gesellschaften Mitteleuropas. Ethnographisch Archäologische Zeitschrift 42: 1-42.

Grout, J.B. 2016. The Role of Palmyrene Temples in Long-Distance Trade in the Roman Near East. Unpublished PhD Dissertation, Classics, University of London.

Guerrero, S. 2010. Venetian Glass Beads and the Slave Trade from Liverpool, 1750-1800. BEADS Journal of the Society of Bead Researchers 22: 52-70.

Guler, K. 2013. The Impact of the Ancient Greek Slave Trade on Art in the Balkans. Saber and Scroll 2 (2), article 4.

Gustafsson, K. 2005. The Trade in Slaves in Ovamboland, ca. 1850-1910. African Economic History 33: 31-68.

Harrill, J.A. 2006. Slaves in the New Testament: Literary, Social, and Moral Dimensions. Minneapolis: Fortress Press.

Harris, W.V. 1999. Demography, Geography and the Sources of Roman Slaves. Journal of Roman Studies 89: 62-75.

Harris, W.V. 2011. Rome's Imperial Economy: Twelve Essays. Oxford: Oxford University Press.

Haselgrove, C. 1984. Warfare and its Aftermath as reflected in the Precious Metal Coinage of Belgic Gaul. Oxford Journal of Archaeology 3 (1): 81-105.

Haselgrove, C. 1987. Culture process on the periphery: Belgic Gaul and Rome during the late republic and early Empire, in M. Rowlands, M. Larsen and K. Kristiansen (eds) Centre and Periphery in the Ancient World: 104-124. Cambridge: Cambridge University Press.

Haselgrove, C. 1999. The Development of Iron Age Coinage in Belgic Gaul. The Numismatic Chronicle 159: 111-168.

Haselgrove, C. 2007. The Age of Enclosure: Later Iron Age Settlement and Society in Northern France, in C. Haselgrove and T.H. Moore (eds) The Later Iron Age in Britain and Beyond: 492-522. Oxford: Oxbow Books.

Hassell, M.W.C. 1970. Batavians and the Roman Conquest of Britain. Britannia 1: 131-136.

Hayden, B. 2003. Were Luxury Foods the First Domesticates? Ethnoarchaeological Perspectives from Southeast Asia. World Archaeology 34 (3): 458-469.

Heath, M. 2008. Aristotle on natural slavery. Phronesis: A Journal for Ancient Philosophy 53 (3): 243 -270.

Henning, J. 1992. Gefangenenfesseln im slawischen Siedlungsraum und der europäische Sklavenhandel im 6. Bis 12. Jahhundert. Germania 70: 403-426.

Hiddink, H. 2014. Cemeteries of the Late Iron Age in the Southern Part of the Netherlands, in A. Cahen-Delhaye and G. de Mulder (eds) Des Espaces aux Esprits. L'organisation de la mort aux âges de Métaux dans le nord-oest de l'Europe. Études et Documents Archéologie 32: 185-212. Namur: Institut du Patrimoine Wallon.

Hill, J.D. 2006. Are we any closer to understanding how later Iron Age societies worked (or did not work)?, in Haselgrove (ed.) Celtes et Gaulois l'archéologie face a l'histoire. Les mutations de la fin de l'Âge du fer. Actes de la table ronde de Cambridge, 7-8 juillet 2005. Collection Bribracte 12/4: 169-179. Glux-en-Glenne: Centre Archéologique Européen.

Hingh, A.E. de 2000. Food production and food procurement in the Bronze Age and Early Iron Age (2000-500 BC). Unpublished PhD Dissertation, Archaeology, University of Leiden.

Hodder, I. (ed.) 1982. Symbolic and Structural Archaeology. Cambridge: Cambridge University Press.

Hodder, I. (ed.) 2007. Revolution Fulfilled? Structural and Symbolic Archaeology a Generation On. Cambridge Archaeological Journal 17 (2): 199-228.

Hopkins, K. 1978. Conquerors and Slaves. Cambridge: Cambridge University Press.

Jankowiak 2013. Two systems of trade in the Western Slavic lands in the 10th century, in M. Bogucki and M. Rębkowski (eds) Economies, Monetisation and Society in the West Slavic Lands 800-1200 AD: 137-148. Szczecin: Institute of Archaeology and Ethnology Polish Academy of Sciences.

Jansen, R., C. van der Linde and H. Fokkens 2002. Archeologisch onderzoek Hertogswetering. Een cultusplaats in de Maaskant. Archol Rapport 7. Leiden University.

Jay, M., C. Haselgrove, D. Hamilton, J.D. Hill and J. Dent 2012. Chariots and Context: New Radiocarbon Dates from Wetwang and the Chronology of Iron Age Burials and brooches in East Yorkshire. Oxford Journal of Archaeology 31 (2): 161-189.

Jongman, W. 2003. Slavery and the growth of Rome: the transformation of Italy in the second and first centuries BCE, in C. Edwards and G. Woolf (eds) Rome the Cosmopolis: 100-122. Cambridge: Cambridge University Press.

Jørgensen, L.B. 1992. North European Textiles until AD 1000. Aarhus: Aarhus University Press.

Joshel, S.R. 2010. Slavery in the Roman World. Cambridge: Cambridge University Press.

Kagan, D. 2003. The Peloponnesian War. New York: Viking.

Kienlin, T.L. 2017. World Systems and the Structuring Potential of Foreign-Derived (Prestige) Goods. On Modelling Bronze Age Economy and Society, in A.K. Scholz, M. Bartelheim, R. Hardenberg and J. Staecker (eds) Resource Cultures. Sociocultural dynamics and the Use of Resources - Theories, Methods, Perspectives: 143-157. Tübingen: Universität Tübingen.

Kincade, K. 2014. The Razor's Edge: Constructing Male Identity in Bronze and Iron Age Northern Europe. Unpublished MA Thesis, Anthropology, University of Wisconsin-Milwaukee.

Kindstedt, P. 2012. Cheese and Culture: A History of Cheese and Its Place in Western Civilization. White River Junction: Chelsea Green Pub.

King, A. 1990. Roman Gaul and Germany. Exploring the Roman World. Berkeley: University of California Press.

Klein, M.A. 2001. The Slave Trade and Decentralized Societies. Journal of African History 42 (1): 49-65.

Kleijwegt, M. 2013. Debt Bondage and Chattel Slavery in early Rome, in G. Campbell and A. Stanziani (eds) Debt and Slavery in the Mediterranean and Atlantic Worlds. Financial History 22: 29-37. London: Routledge.

Koester, C.R. 2008. Roman Slave Trade and the Critique of Babylon in Revelation 18. Catholic Biblical Quarterly 70 (4): 766-786.

Korpela, J. 2014. The Baltic Finnic People in the Medieval and Pre-Modern Eastern European Slave Trade. Russian History 41: 85-117.

Krämer, R.P. 2016. Trading Goods - Trading Gods. Greek Sanctuaries in the Mediterranean and their Role as emporia and 'Ports of Trade' (7th-6th Century BCE), in H. Albery, P. Lohmann and L. Zurhake (eds) Continuities and Changes of Meaning. Distant Worlds Journal 1: 75-98. Heidelberg: Universität Heidelberg.

Kristiansen, K. 1998. Europe Before History. New Studies in Archaeology. Cambridge: Cambridge University Press.

Kusimba, C.M. 2004. Archaeology of Slavery in east Africa. African Archaeological Review 21 (2): 59-88.

Kusimba, C.M. 2015. The Impact of Slavery on the East African Political Economy and Gender Relationships, in L.W. Marshall (ed.) The Archaeology of Slavery: A Comparative Approach to Captivity and Coercion. Center for Archaeological Investigations Southern Illinois University Carbondale Occasional Paper 41: 230-254. Carbondale: Southern Illinois University Press.

Laes, C. 2011. Children in the Roman Empire: Outsiders Within. Cambridge: Cambridge University Press.

Lane, P. and K.C. MacDonald (eds) 2011. Slavery in Africa: Archaeology and Memory. London: British Academy.

Lavan, M. 2013. Slaves to Rome: Paradigms of Empire in Roman Culture. Cambridge Classical Studies. Cambridge: Cambridge University Press.

Leeuwe, R. de, and R. Jansen 2018. Space becomes a ritualized place. Five Iron Age and Early Roman period presumed cult places in Oss (The Netherlands), in E.A.G. Ball, R. Jansen, E.H.L.D. Norde and K.M. de Vries (eds) Metaaltijden. Bijdragen in de Studie van de Metaaltijden 5: 175-190. Leiden: Sidestone Press.

Lejars, T. 2012. The Golden Age of the Celtic Aristocracy in the Fourth and Third Centuries BC. Annales. Histoire, Sciences Sociales 67 (2): 185-215.

Lenski, N. 2008. Captivity, Slavery, and Cultural Exchange between Rome and the Germans from the First to the Seventh Century CE, in C.M. Cameron (ed.) Invisible Citizens: Captives and Their Consequences: 80–109. Salt Lake City: University of Utah Press.

Lewis, D.M. 2011. Near eastern Slaves in Classical Attica and the Slave Trade with Persian Territories. Classical Quarterly 61 (1): 91-113.

Lewis, D.M. 2015. The Market for Slaves in the Fifth and Fourth Century Aegean: Achaemenid Anatolia as a Case Study, in E.M. Harris, D.M. Lewis and M. Woolmer (eds) The Ancient Greek Economy: Markets, Households and City-States: 316-336. Cambridge: Cambridge University Press.

Loughton, M. 2009. Getting Smashed: The Deposition of Amphorae and the Drinking of Wine in Gaul during the Late Iron Age. Oxford Journal of Archaeology 28 (1): 77-110.

MacEachern, S. 2011. Enslavement and Everyday Life: Living with Slave Raiding in the North-Eastern Mandara Mountains of Cameroon. Proceedings of the British Academy 168: 109-124.

Markey, T. 2013. 'Garlic and Sapphires in the Mud': 'Leeks' in their Early Folk Contexts, in C. Biggam (ed.) *Magic and Medicine. Early Medieval Plant-Name Studies.* Leeds Studies in English. New Series XLIV: 10-42. Leeds: University of Leeds.

Marshall, L. W. (ed.) 2015. The Archaeology of Slavery: A Comparative Approach to Captivity and Coercion. Center for Archaeological Investigations Southern Illinois University Carbondale Occasional Paper 41. Carbondale: Southern Illinois University Press.

Martin, D.L and N.J. Akins 2001. Unequal Treatment in Life as in Death: Trauma and Mortuary Behavior at La Plata (A.D. 1000-1300), in D.R. Mitchell and J.L Brunson-Hadley (eds) Ancient Burial Practices in the American Southwest: 223-248. Albuquerque: University of New Mexico Press.

Mata, K. 2012. Anthropological Perspectives on Colonialism, Globalization and Rural Lifeways: Expanding the Limits of Archaeological Interpretation in the Lower Rhineland, in M. Duggan, F. McIntosh and D.J. Rohl (eds) TRAC 2011: Proceedings of the Twenty First Annual Theoretical Roman Archaeology Conference in Newcastle (UK) 14-17 April 2011: 33-47. Oxford: Oxbow Books.

Mata, K. 2017a. Of Barbarians and Boundaries: The making and remaking of Transcultural Discourse, in S. González Sánchez and A. Guglielmi (eds) Romans and 'barbarians' beyond the frontiers: Archaeology, Ideology and Identities in the North. Theoretical Roman Archaeology Conference. Themes in Roman Archaeology 1: 8-33. Oxford: Oxbow Books.

Mata, K. 2017b. Values Materialized: An Interdisciplinary Archaeology of Socio-Historical Transformation in the Celto-Germanic Iron Age and Roman Period. Unpublished PhD Dissertation, Anthropology, University of Chicago.

McCormick 2002. New Light on the 'Dark Ages': How the Slave Trade Fuelled the Carolingian Economy. Past and Present 177 (1): 17-54.

Michael, S.M. 2003. Meaning and significance of feasts and festivals in human society. Journal of Dharma 28 (3): 366-376.

Miller, J.C. 2008. Slaving as a historical process: examples from the ancient Mediterranean and the modern Atlantic, in E. Dal Lago and C. Katsari (eds) Slave Systems: Ancient and Modern: 70-102. Cambridge: Cambridge University Press.

Miller, D. and C.Y. Tilley (eds) 1984. Ideology, Power, and Prehistory. Cambridge: Cambridge University Press.

Moghaddam, N., S. Mailler-Burch, L. Kara, F. Kanz, C. Jackowski and S. Lösch 2015. Survival after trepanation – Early cranial surgery from Late Iron Age Switzerland. International Journal of Paleopathology 11: 56-65.

Moore, T. and X.L. Armada (eds) 2011. Atlantic Europe in the First Millennium BC: Crossing the Divide. Oxford: Oxford University Press.

Moore, T., A. Braun, J. Creighton, L. Cripps, P. Haupt, I. Klenner, P. Nouvel, C. Ponroy and M. Schönfelder 2013. Oppida, Agglomerations, and Suburbia: the Bibracte Environs and New Perspectives on Late Iron Age Urbanism in Central-Eastern France. European Journal of Archaeology 44: 491–517.

Morris, F.M. 2010. North Sea and Channel Connectivity during the Late Iron Age and Roman Period (175/150 BC - AD 409). British Archaeological Reports International Series 2157. Oxford: BAR Publishing.

Morteani, G. and J.P. Northover 1995. Prehistoric Gold in Europe: Mines, Metallurgy, and Manufacture. NATO advanced research workshop on prehistoric gold in Europe, held at Seeon, Germany, from September 26 to October 1, 1993. NATO Advanced Study Institutes. Series E. Applied Sciences 280. Dordrecht: Kluwer Academic.

Mulder, G. de and J. Bourgeois 2011. Shifting Centres of Power and Changing Elite Symbolism in the Scheldt Fluvial Basin during the Late Bronze Age and the Iron Age, in T. Moore and X.-L. Armada (eds) Atlantic Europe in the First Millenium BC. Crossing the Divide: 302-318. Oxford: Oxford University Press.

Murphy, E.M. (ed.) 2008. Deviant Burial in the Archaeological Record. Oxford: Oxbow Books.

Murray, M.L. 1995. Viereckschanzen and feasting: Socio-political ritual in Iron-Age central Europe. Journal of European Archaeology 3 (2): 125-151.

Murray, M.L. 2004. Viereckschanzen, in P. Bogucki and P.J. Crabtree (eds) Ancient Europe. 8000 B.C. – A.D. 1000. Encyclopedia of the Barbarian World. Volume II. Bronze Age to Early Middle Ages (c. 3000 B.C. – A.D. 1000): 175-178. New York: Thompson Gale.

Nash, D. 1985. Celtic Territorial Expansion and the Mediterranean World, in T.C. Champion and J.V.S. Megaw (eds) Settlement and Society: Aspects of Western European Prehistory in the First Millennium BC: 46-67. Leicester: Leicester University Press.

Nash-Briggs, D. 2002. Servants at a Rich Man's Feast: Early Etruscan Household Slaves and Their Procurement. Etruscan Studies 9 (14): 153-176.

Nash-Briggs, D. 2003. Metals, Salt, and Slaves: Economic Links between Gaul and Italy from the Eighth to the Late Sixth Centuries BC. Oxford Journal of Archaeology 22 (3): 243-259.

Neth, A. and K. Schatz 1996. Grabungen in einer spatkeltischen Viereckschanze in Nordheim, Kr. Heilbronn. Denkmalpflege in Baden-Württemberg 25: 131-139.

Nicolai, C. von 2006. Sacral oder profan? Späteisenzeitliche Einfriedungen in Nordfrankreich und Süddeutschland, in S. Rieckhoff and W.-R. Teegen (eds) Leipziger online-Beiträge zur Ur- und Frühgeschichtlichen Archäologie 22. Leipzig: Universität Leipzig.

Nicolai, C. von 2009. La question des Viereckschanzen d'Allemagne du Sud revisitée, in I. Bertrand, A. Duval, J. Gomez de Soto and P. Maguer (eds) Habitats et paysages ruraux en Gaule et regards sur d'autres régions du monde celtique. Actes du XXXIe colloque international de l'Association Francaise pour l'Étude de l'Âge du Fer. 17-20 mai 2007, Chauvigny (Vienne, France). Volume II: 245-280.

Nosch, M.-L. B. 2001. Kinderarbeit in der mykenischen Palastzeit, in J. Borchhardt and F. Krinzinger (eds) Akten des Östereichischen Archäologentages am Institut for Klassische Archäologie der Universität Wien vom 23. Bis 25. April 1999. Wiener Forschungen zur Archäologie 4: 37-43. Wien: Phoibos Verlag.

Nosch, M.-L. B. 2014. The Aegean Wool Economies of the Bronze Age. Textile Society of America 2014 Biennial Symposium Proceedings: New Directions: Examining the Past, Creating the Future, Los Angeles, California, September 10-14, 2014: 1-13. Lincoln: University of Nebraska.

Nussbaum, M. C. 2018. The Monarchy of Fear. A Philosopher Looks at Our Political Crisis. Oxford: Oxford University Press.

Nwokeji, G. U. 2010. The Slave Trade and Culture in the Bight of Biafra: An African Society in the Atlantic World. Cambridge: Cambridge University Press.

Oelze, V.M. 2012. Mobility and Diet in Neolithic, Bronze Age and Iron Age Germany: Evidence from Multiple Isotope Analysis. Unpublished PhD Dissertation, Archaeology, Leiden University.

Oelze, V.M., J.K. Koch, K. Kupke, O. Nehlich, S. Zäuner, J. Wahl, S. M. Weise, S. Rieckhoff and M.P. Richards 2012. Multi-Isotopic Analysis reveals Individual Mobility and Diet at the early Iron Age Monumental Tumulus of Madalenenberg, Germany. American Journal of Physical Anthropology 148: 406-421.

Ojo, O. 2005. Slavery and Human Sacrifice in Yorubaland: Ondo, c. 1870-94. Journal of African History 46 (3): 379-404.

Olson, K. 2008. Dress and the Roman Woman: Self-Presentation and Society. London: Routledge.

Ortner, S.B. 2005. Subjectivity and cultural critique. Anthropological Theory 5 (1): 31-52.

Patterson, O. 1982. Slavery and Social Death: A Comparative Study. Cambridge: Harvard University Press.

Patterson, O. 2008. Slavery, Gender, and Work in the Pre-Modern World and Early Greece: A Cross-Cultural Analysis, in E. Dal Lago and C. Katsari (eds) Slave Systems: Ancient and Modern: 32-69. Cambridge: Cambridge University Press.

Perego, E. 2014. Anomalous Mortuary Behaviour and Social Exclusion in Iron Age Italy: A Case Study from the Veneto Region. Journal of Mediterranean Archaeology 27 (2): 161-186.

Peregrine, P.N. 2001. Cross-Cultural Comparative Approaches in Archaeology. Annual Review of Anthropology 30 (1): 1-18.

Peschel, K. 1971. Zur Frage der Sklaverei bei den Kelten während der vorrömischen Eisenzeit. Ethnographisch Archäologische Zeitschrift 12: 527-539.

Pomeroy, S.B. 1975. Goddesses, Whores, Wives, and Slaves: Women in Classical Antiquity. New York: Schocken Books.

Pope, R. and I. Ralston 2011. Approaching Sex and Status in Iron Age Britain with Reference to the Nearer Continent, in T. Moore and X.L. Armada (eds) Atlantic Europe in the First Millennium BC: Crossing the Divide: 375-414. Oxford: Oxford University Press.

Rauh, N.K. 1993. The Sacred Bonds of Commerce: Religion, Economy, and Trade Society at Hellenistic Roman Delos, 166-87 B.C. Amsterdam: J.C. Gieben.

Robertshaw, P. and W.L. Duncan 2008. African Slavery: Archaeology and Decentralized Societies, in C.M. Cameron (ed.) Invisible Citizens: Captives and Their Consequences: 57-79. Salt Lake City: University of Utah Press.

Robinson, E.W. 2008. Ancient Greek Democracy Readings and Sources. Interpreting Ancient History. Hoboken: Wiley.

Rosivach, V.J. 1999. Enslaving "Barbaroi" and the Athenian Ideology of Slavery. Historia 48 (2): 129-157.

Rowlands, M.J, M.T. Larsen and K. Kristiansen (eds) 1987. Centre and Periphery in the Ancient World. New Directions in Archaeology. Cambridge: Cambridge University Press.

Rowlett, R.M. 1988. Titelberg. A Celtic Hillfort in Luxembourg. Expedition Magazine 30 (2): 31-40.

Roymans, N. 1990. Tribal Societies in Northern Gaul: An Anthropological Perspective. Amsterdam: Institute for Pre-and Protohistoric Archaeology Albert Egges van Giffen.

Roymans, N. 1996. The Sword or the Plough. Regional Dynamics in the Romanisation of Belgic Gaul and the Rhineland Area, in N. Roymans (ed.) From the Sword to the Plough: Three Studies on the Earliest Romanisation of Northern Gaul. Amsterdam Archaeological Studies 1: 9-126. Amsterdam: Amsterdam University Press.

Roymans, N. 2004. Ethnic Identity and Imperial Power: The Batavians in the Early Roman Empire. Amsterdam Archaeological Studies 10. Amsterdam: Amsterdam University Press.

Roymans, N. 2007. Understanding Social Change in the Late Iron Age Lower Rhine Region, in C. Haselgrove and T.H. Moore (eds) The Later Iron Age in Britain and Beyond: 478-491. Oxford: Oxbow Books.

Roymans, N. 2009. Hercules and the Construction of a Batavian Identity in the Context of the Roman Empire, in T. Derks and N. Roymans (eds) Ethnic Constructs in Antiquity: The Role of Power and Tradition: 219-238. Amsterdam: Amsterdam University Press.

Roymans, N. and J. Aarts 2009. Tribal emission or imperial coinage? Ideas about the production and circulation of the so-called AVAVCIA coinages in the Rhineland, in J. van Heesch and I. Heeren (eds) Coinage in the Iron Age. Essays in honour of Simone Scheers: 1-17. London: Spink & Son Ltd.

Roymans and Habermehl 2011. On the Origin and development of axial villas with double courtyards in the Latin West, in N. Roymans and T. Derks (eds) Villa Landscapes in the Roman North. Economy, Culture and Lifestyles. Amsterdam Archaeological Studies 17: 83-106. Amsterdam: Amsterdam University Press.

Roymans, N. and L. Verniers 2010. Glass La Tène Bracelets in the Lower Rhine Region. Typology, Chronology and Social Interpretation. Germania 88: 195-219.

Roymans, N., H. Huisman, J. van der Laan and B. van Os 2014. La Tène Glass Armrings in Europe. Interregional Connectivity and Local Identity Construction. Archäologisches Korrespondenzblatt 44 (2): 215-228.

Sacchetti, F. 2016. Transport Amphorae in the West Hallstatt Zone: Reassessing Socio-Economic Dynamics and Long-Distance Mediterranean Exchange in Western Central Europe in the Early Iron Age. Oxford Journal of Archaeology 35 (3): 247-265.

Sastre, I. 2011. Social Inequality during the Iron Age. Interpretation Models, in T. Moore and X.L. Armada (eds) Atlantic Europe in the First Millennium BC: Crossing the Divide: 264-284. Oxford: Oxford University Press.

Scheeres, M. 2014. High mobility rates during the period of the "Celtic migrations"? 87Sr/86Sr and δ18O evidence from Early La Tène Europe. Unpublished PhD Dissertation, Biology, Universität Mainz.

Scheeres, M., C. Knipper, M. Hauschild, M. Schönfelder, W. Siebel, D. Vitali, C. Pare and K.W. Alt 2013. Evidence for "Celtic migrations"? Strontium isotope analysis at the early La Tène (LT B) cemeteries of Nebringen (Germany) and Monte Bibele (Italy). Journal of Archaeological Science 40: 3614-3625.

Scheidel, W. 1997. Quantifying the Sources of Slaves in the Early Roman Empire. Journal of Roman Studies 87: 156-169.

Scheidel, W. 2011. The Roman slave supply, in K. Bradley and P. Cartledge (eds) The Cambridge World History of Slavery 1: The ancient Mediterranean world. Cambridge: Cambridge University Press: 287-310.

Scheidel, W. 2008. The Comparative Economics of Slavery in the Greco-Roman World, in E. Dal Lago and C. Katsari (eds) Slave Systems: Ancient and Modern: 105-126. Cambridge: Cambridge University Press.

Schneider, J. 1987. The Anthropology of Cloth. Annual Review of Anthropology 16: 409-448.

Schönfelder, M. 2015. Sklaven und Sklavenketten in der jüngeren Latènezeit: zu neuen Nachweismöglichkeiten, in S. Wefers, M. Karwowski, J. Fries-Knoblach, P. Trebsche and P.C. Ramsl (eds) Waffen – Gewalt – Krieg. Beiträge Internationalen. Tagung der AG Eisenzeit und des Instytut Archeologii Uniwersytetu Rzeszowskiego – Rzeszów 19-22 September 2012. Beiträge zur Ur- und Frühgeschichte Mitteleuropas 79: 83-91.

Schörle, K. 2012. Saharan Trade in Classical Antiquity, in J. McDougall and J. Scheele (eds) Saharan Frontiers: Space and Mobility in Northwest Africa: 58-72. Bloomington: Indiana University Press.

Shaw, M.L. 2007. The North Smelter at Titelberg: Post-Imperial Bronze Recycling in Belgic Gaul. Unpublished MA Thesis, Anthropology, University of Missouri.

Shefton, B.B. 1995. Leaven in the dough: Greek and Etruscan imports north of the Alps in the Classical period, in J. Swaddling, S. Walker and P. Roberts (eds) Italy in Europe: Economic Relations 700 BC - AD 50: 9-44. London: British Museum.

Sicherl, B. 2007. Eisenzeitliche Befestigungen in Westfalen, in S. Müller, W. Schlüter and S. Sievers (eds) Keltische Einflüsse im nördlichen Mitteleuropa während der mittleren und jüngeren vorrömischen Eisenzeit. Akten des internationalen Kolloquiums in Osnabrück 2006 (Bonn 2007). Römisch-Germanische Kommission des Deutschen Archäologischen Instituts: 107-151. Frankfurt: Köthen.

Sievers, S. 1999. Manching: Aufstieg Und Niedergang Einer Keltenstadt. Bericht Der Römisch Germanischen Kommission 80: 5-23.

Silver, M. 1992. Taking Ancient Mythology Economically. Leiden: Brill.

Silver, M. 2011. Contractual Slavery in the Roman Economy. Ancient History Bulletin 25: 73-132.

Sîrbu, V. 2008. Ritual Inhumations and 'Deposits' of Children among the Geto-Dacians, in E.M. Murphy (ed.) Deviant Burial in the Archaeological Record: 71-90. Oxford: Oxbow Books.

Snyder, C. 2012. Slavery in Indian Country: The Changing Face of Captivity in Early America. Cambridge: Harvard University Press.

Spielmann, K.A. 2002. Feasting, Craft Specialization, and the Ritual Mode of Production in Small-Scale Societies. American Anthropologist New Series 104 (1): 195-207.

Stahl, A.B. 2008. The Slave Trade as Practice and Memory: What Are the Issues for Archaeologists?, in C.M. Cameron (ed.) Invisible Citizens: Captives and Their Consequences: 25-56. Salt Lake City: University of Utah Press.

Taylor, A. 2008. Aspects of Deviant Burial in Roman Britain, in E.M. Murphy (ed.) Deviant Burial in the Archaeological Record: 91-114. Oxford: Oxbow Books.

Taylor, T. 2001. Believing the ancients: Quantitative and qualitative dimensions of slavery and the slave trade in prehistoric Eurasia. World Archaeology 33 (1): 27-43.

Taylor, T. 2005. Ambushed by a grotesque: archaeology, slavery and the third paradigm, M. Parker Pearson and I.J. Thorpe (eds) Warfare, Violence and Slavery in Prehistory: Proceedings of a Prehistoric Society Conference at Sheffield University. British Archaeological Reports International Series 1374: 225-233. Oxford: BAR Publishing.

Tchernia, A. 1983. Italian Wine in Gaul at the end of the Republic, in P. Garnsey, K. Hopkins and C.R. Whittaker (eds) Trade in the Ancient Economy: 87-104. Berkeley: University of California Press.

Thompson, E.A. 1957. Slavery in Early Germany. Hermathena 89: 17-29.

Thompson, F. H. 1993. Iron Age and Roman Slave-Shackles. Archaeological Journal 150 (1): 57-168.

Torelli, M. 2000. The Etruscan City-State, in M.H. Hansen (ed.) A Comparative Study of Thirty City-State Cultures: An Investigation: 189-208. Copenhagen: Kongelige Danske Videnskabernes Selskab.

Vaart-Verschoof, S. van der, 2017. Fragmenting the Chieftain. A practice-based study of Early Iron Age Hallstatt C elite burials in the Low Countries. Papers on Archaeology of the Leiden Museum of Antiquities 15. Leiden: Sidestone Press.

Vaart-Verschoof, S. van der, and R. Schumann 2017. Differentiation and globalization in Early Iron Age Europe. Reintegrating the early Hallstatt period (Ha C) into the debate, in R. Schumann and S. van der Vaart-Verschoof (eds) Connecting Elites and Regions. Perspectives on contacts, relations and differentiation during the Early Iron Age Hallstatt C period in Northwest and Central Europe: 9-27. Leiden: Sidestone Press.

Vandemoortele, K. 2011. Late La Tène oppida in West and Central Europe. Unpublished PhD Dissertation, History and Archaeology, Cardiff University.

Veldman, H.A.P. 2003. Fossiel Verleden: het gebruik van barnsteen in de Romeinse tijd. Unpublished MA Thesis, Archaeology, University of Amsterdam.

Vencl, S. 1994. The archaeology of thirst. Journal of European Archaeology 2 (2): 299-326.

Verhoeven, M.P.F. 2008. Studieopdracht naar een archeologische evaluatie van het plateau van Caestert (Riemst, Provincie Limburg). RAAP-rapport 1769. Weesp: RAAP Archeologisch Adviesbureau B.V.

Vleeshouwer, F.L. 2012. Inhumatiegraven uit de vroege en midden ijzertijd in het Nederlandse riverengebied. Unpublished BA Thesis, Archaeology, Universiteit Leiden.

Walsh, J. 2014. Consumerism in the Ancient World: Imports and Identity Construction. Routledge Monographs in Classical Studies 17. New York: Routledge.

Waterbolk, H.T. 1977. Walled Enclosures of the Iron Age in the North of the Netherlands. Palaeohistoria 19: 97-172.

Watson, T. 2018. Prehistoric children toiled at tough tasks. Nature 561, 27 September: 445-446.

Webster, J. 2008. Less beloved. Roman archaeology, slavery and the failure to compare. Archaeological Dialogues 15 (2): 103-123.

Wells, P.S. 1999. The Barbarians Speak: How the Conquered Peoples Shaped Roman Europe. Princeton: Princeton University Press.

Wells, P.S. 2002. The Iron Age, in S. Milisauskas (ed.) European Prehistory: A Survey: 335-387. New York: Kluwer Academic/Plenum Publishers.

Wells, P.S. 2005. Creating an Imperial Frontier: Archaeology of the Formation of Rome's Danube Borderland. Journal of Archaeological Research 13 (1): 49-88.

Wells, P.S. 2012. How Ancient Europeans Saw the World: Vision, Patterns, and the Shaping of the Mind in Prehistoric Times. Princeton: Princeton University Press.

Wiedmer, H.R. 1963. Menschliche Skelettreste au Spätlatène-Siedlungen im Alpenvorland. Germania 41: 269-317.

Wild, J.P. 1976. The Gynaecea, in JR. Goodburn and P. Bartholomew (eds) Aspects of the Notitia Dignitatum. Papers presented to the conference in Oxford, December 13 to 15, 1974. British Archaeological reports Supplementary series 15: 51-58. Oxford: BAR Publishing.

Wilson, A. 2012. Saharan trade in the Roman period: short-, medium- and long-distance trade networks. Azania: Archaeological Research in Africa 47 (4): 409-449.

Wit, M.J.M de 1997/1998. Elite in Drenthe? Een analyse van twaalf opmerkelijke drentse graf-inventarissen uit de vroege en het begin van de midden-ijzertijd. Palaeohistoria 39/40: 323-373.

Woolf, G. 1993. Rethinking the Oppida. Oxford Journal of Archaeology 12 (2): 223-234.

Wrenhaven, K. 2013. Barbarians at the Gate: Foreign Slaves in Greek City-States. Electryone 1 (1): 1-17.

Zeuske, M. 2012. Historiography and Research Problems of Slavery and the Slave Trade in a Global-Historical Perspective. International Review of Social History 57: 87-111.